MW00897299

"...one of the chiefe trees or postes at the right side

of the entrance had the barke taken off, and 5

foote from the ground in fayre Capital letters was

C R O A T O A N

graven in the Roman

without any crosse or any signe of distress."

John White, 5th Voyage

Mystery of the Lost Colony

The Untold Story of Survival

CROATAN

by William V. Pate, Sr., & Wanda Herring

Copyright© 2013
ISBN: 978-1-300-74939-4

by William V. Pate, Sr. & Wanda Herring

All Rights Reserved. No part of this book may be used or
reproduced in any manner whatsoever without written permission
except in the case of brief quotations used in articles and reviews.

Printed and bound in the United States of America

For information, visit our website at
www.sharpandshulerpress.com

or email us at
sharp-shulerpress@hotmail.com

Edited by Jacquelyn Brown
Cover design by Jacquelyn Brown
Technical Support by David Herring

Dedication

With great admiration this book is dedicated to you men, women, and children of the Lost Colony, the first English to arrive upon the shores of North America determined to establish a permanent home. Stepping ashore in the land then called Virginia, you claimed forever the distinction of being the first citizens of English blood to call this country home.

Brave and determined, you readily accepted the challenges of a long, dangerous sea voyage across crudely charted waters aboard small, crowded ships. You came to this newfound land in high spirits, with worthy dreams, and in the hope that you would open the way for others to follow. When your great undertaking was threatened by events unknown to you and by circumstances beyond your control, your hopes and dreams could not be fulfilled in the way you imagined.

In the years without contact from your mother country, your rugged faith in God sustained you, your instinct for survival strengthened you, and the devotion of your Native American friends encouraged you. Together you slipped quietly out of the view of history, presenting this nation with one of its most enduring and treasured mysteries.

Author's Preface

by William V. Pate, Sr.

As a youngster growing up in the southern part of Cumberland County, North Carolina three-quarters of a century ago, one of my favorite pastimes was searching for artifacts of long gone generations of American Indians. My friends and I spent many happy hours searching for the best places to dig and still more hours scratching in the earth with stout sticks, sharp rocks, or anything useful in turning over the soil. Mostly what we found were bits of clay pottery with the Indian "corn on the cob" pattern. Little did we understand the true significance of our treasures. Both the distinctive pattern made by pressing an ear of corn into damp clay, as well as the type of pottery, could prove useful to trained researchers in dating our finds.

What every boy really hoped to discover was stone arrowheads. We usually found arrowheads intact, and they conjured up in our imaginations great battles between cowboys and Indians, or adventurous young braves out on the hunt for wild game. As we examined the workmanship of the arrowheads in our hands, I wish we had known that the shape of the stone indicated the approximate date it was crafted, and the type of stone indicated the area of the country from whence it came. We had no idea that the stone arrowheads represented a leap of progress from an age five thousand years ago. At that time Indians fashioned arrows from very dense wood that had been hardened by heat and then sharpened to a point.

But as boys our ideas of Indians were what we learned from the western movies when we had a spare dime, and the stories we listened to about the Indians in Robeson County. I remember hearing of Robeson County Indians who had blonde hair, blue eyes, spoke English, and claimed to be descendants of the English of the Lost Colony. This was certainly at odds with the depiction of Indians in the movies. I was more than a little confused when the history taught in our schools indicated that all of the English people of the Lost Colony were massacred by the forces of King Powhatan of "Virginia". This account from the Jamestown Colony twenty years after the settlement of the Lost Colony was accepted as fact. Even as a boy, I was aware that there was a conflict in history.

Through the years as I observed the Indians in Robeson County, known as Croatans, I wondered many times about this conflict and what the real truth might be. About 1975, I was so intrigued with the mystery that my hobby became searching for the answers. My search revealed that many researchers and writers do not agree with the theory of massacre by King Powhatan. Some believe it more likely that they were slaughtered instead by local hostile Indians. Others blame the demise of the colony on starvation due to a great drought, or perhaps the colonists built a ship and attempted to return to England, likely perishing at sea. It seemed to me that none of these theories was supported by compelling evidence.

I found a substantial amount of recorded information pertinent to the Lost Colony beginning in 1584 with the First Voyage to the coast of America, sponsored by Sir Walter Raleigh, until the time of the disappearance of the colonists from Roanoke Island prior to 1590. When Governor John White departed his colony in 1587, the colonists were never again in contact with fellow Englishmen. From that time until approximately 1700, when there were reports from other colonists and explorers of encountering English-speaking people of "mixed breed," information is quite limited. It is the belief of this author that several pieces of evidence provide enough clues to the insightful researcher to conclude that the colony planted on Roanoke Island, N.C., in the year 1587 did indeed survive. My study revealed oral information passed down from generation to generation that supports the survival of the colonists. While some may dismiss oral tradition as unreliable, it has been the only means of preserving the history and tradition of cultures without a written language. Simply because these histories are not committed to writing is not an acceptable reason to disbelieve them.

No less a publication than National Geographic Magazine is a perfect case in point. Some twenty years ago, National Geographic Magazine presented a detailed article about the American Indians and their place of origin. There was no written record, but it was the conclusion of the magazine that the people crossed from Asia to the American Continent using a land bridge that connected the two land masses.

The crossing was believed to have been some fourteen thousand years ago. When the natives were interviewed and asked the question as to the origin of their ancestors, they most often said, "from the direction of the setting sun". If that oral tradition survived for thousands of years to be accepted as fact, should not that of only 400 years ago be even more reliable as it has had much less time for exposure to adulteration?

Since much has been written in support of the idea that the colony planted in 1587 was completely lost, those theories will not be the focus of this book. Instead, recorded history, oral traditions, and archeological discoveries will be presented to support the assertion that the colonists did indeed survive and can be connected to the Lumbee Indians of Roberson County, N.C., as well as other areas. DNA testing is now under way to determine any conclusive link. It may be years before DNA testing is complete, but in the meantime, this author believes that when the evidence is impartially considered it overwhelmingly supports survival. The reader may consider the body of evidence presented here and draw his own conclusion.

The English colony founded on the shore of North Carolina in 1587 has been called the "establishment of English America," and it deserves a far greater place in the history not only of North Carolina, but in the history of the United States. It is my belief that it is the fountainhead of our nation.

My hope is that this book may inspire a more careful study of the facts and encourage historians to give the Lost Colony and its brave colonists the prominent place they deserve in our nation's history.

William V. Pate, Sr.

Author's Preface

by Wanda Herring

I come by my fascination with solving mysteries naturally. My father was a detective and a people watcher. When I was growing up, one of his favorite pastimes was to drive the family to the main street of town, buy everyone ice cream cones, and sit back to watch the parade. For every person who passed by, my father would give us a complete rundown on his idea of who they probably were, where they had been and where they were going. He noticed everything from the cut of their hair to the shine on their shoes, and was so adept at weaving his stories that they seemed believable.

As we sat around the table at supper, he would entertain us with stories based very loosely on the people involved in his cases. There was lots of exaggeration to create a compelling story, but I learned that the best skill a detective can have is a good understanding of human nature and how it determines a person's actions. Human nature doesn't change, and it is part of every mystery. Today, insight into human nature is a large part of what is known as "profiling", or how a particular individual is likely to act in a certain set of circumstances.

I'm not alone in my love of mysteries. Good mystery books are always on the best-seller lists, and new mystery shows seem to be included in every television season.

Today the technology for solving mysteries seems to outpace our ability to keep up with all of it. And yet one of our nation's greatest mysteries remains unsolved after more than four hundred years. Like all unsolved mysteries, the passage of time diminishes the likelihood that it will ever be solved to everyone's satisfaction. Hard evidence becomes degraded, reports and documents are misplaced or lost, testimonies are no longer contemporary, and people lose interest if there is no ongoing progress.

When Sir Walter Raleigh's colony on Roanoke Island, N.C. "disappeared" from history in 1587, it was three years before anyone noticed it was missing. The scene was no longer fresh; clues had likely been swept away by wind and waves; the witnesses had moved on. One of the greatest obstacles to solving this mystery has been that no skilled investigators ever inspected the scene or the evidence left behind when it was discovered that the colony was no longer on Roanoke Island. Although it had been three years since they were last seen and evidence would not have been fresh, it would have been more revealing than it can ever be after the passage of hundreds of years.

In order to solve this mystery, we can no longer start at the scene and work outward in ever increasing circles to examine the evidence. Most of it has been obliterated by time. No, if we are to solve this mystery we must come at it from many different angles, assembling whatever clues we can find like a jigsaw puzzle.

Some of the pieces of the puzzle will be missing and perhaps waiting to be discovered at a later date. A few pieces will have faded so that we have to look at the surrounding pieces to make any sense of them. Some may even be broken, but there are just enough perfect pieces to provide us with the overall picture.

In our investigation, we shall examine the hard evidence of recorded history including legal documents, maps, letters and journals. That is a good foundation, but it is not enough. We shall also consider the "nature" of the participants in this mystery. Since the Indians involved had no written language to preserve events, we shall consider their oral tradition. As oral tradition was the only way they had to pass on their history from generation to generation, they took it seriously and so should we. Using all of these resources, we shall be able to make reasonable assumptions in solving one of our nation's greatest mysteries.

Wanda Herring

Table of Contents

Page

Table of Contents

Chapter 1

The Age of Exploration

The intriguing story of the survival of the Lost Colony presented in this book is best understood when considered from two different points of view. The first point of view is based on the factual recorded history of the time beginning with discovery by Christopher Columbus in 1492 of the new world he called America, through the year 1590, when recorded information of the Lost Colony ended. The second point of view takes into account the value of various pertinent events, significant discoveries, oral history and cultural heritage. While the first point of view is influenced solely by hard, cold facts which historians prefer, the second point of view continues to gain increasing acceptance as investigators better understand the importance of circumstantial evidence and common sense in making reasonable connections to reach a valid conclusion.

With the discovery of this New World across the vast sea, Spain's interest in expanding its empire intensified. Spanish expeditions concentrated on the area of present-day Central America and Mexico. To their astonishment, the explorers came in contact with people of advanced cultures. Their cities contained stone houses and streets laid out in an orderly manner. The Spanish explorers were impressed with the abundant use of gold to decorate temples and homes of the rulers.

So much treasure was impossible for the Spanish to resist, and they quickly began raiding these buildings for gold to send back to Spain. They also located the mines where the gold was obtained and took it to fill their treasure ships.

With gold pouring in from the New World, Spain concentrated on becoming a more powerful nation by building a strong military force with a great number of ships. This newfound revenue and the resulting military buildup did not escape the notice of Spain's great enemy, England. England was not pleased with this challenge to its status as military and commercial leader in Europe. As a Protestant nation, England also feared that the growing strength of Spain could lead to a spreading influence of the Catholic Church.

Queen Elizabeth I realized the importance of obtaining a presence in North America before Spain got a foothold there. The Queen decided to accomplish this by issuing charters to persons of her choosing to establish colonies in North America. Her plan stipulated the funds for the ventures would come from private investors, not the English government. This approach to exploration and colonization would have a great influence on future events.

On March 25, 1584, Queen Elizabeth issued a charter to Sir Walter Raleigh, authorizing the planting of a colony or colonies in the area of North America from 33 to 40 degrees of latitude, the area which would become known as "Virginia", in honor of the Virgin Queen.

In the year 1584, Sir Walter Raleigh sent explorers in two ships across the Atlantic Ocean to the shores of North America. The ships found a safe harbor in the northeast area of present-day North Carolina. After a brief visit in which they met the native people and did reconnaissance of the area, they returned to England. Accompanying the explorers back to England were two native men, Manteo and Wanchese. These Indians spent almost one year in England observing the many wonders of a modern nation.

In the year 1585, a colony of a little over one hundred men and the two Indians arrived on Roanoke Island and established their dwelling place. These men remained almost one year while they built necessary buildings, explored the greater area around them, including the sounds, the rivers, and the location of native villages. During this time they had the opportunity to observe the culture of the native people and gain a better understanding of the challenges of planting a permanent colony. These men returned to England in the year 1586. Shortly after their departure ships arrived with supplies, but not finding the men present on the island the ships returned to England. There were two separate attempts to resupply the colony on Roanoke Island, but both arrived after the colonists had already sailed for England.

In the year 1587, another colony consisting of 117 men, women and children arrived and took up dwelling on Roanoke Island in the houses built by the men of the Second Voyage. They named their village "Cittie of Raleigh".

Having arrived at Roanoke the twenty second of July, the colonists soon realized that their arrival was too late in the season for growing vegetables. Their supply of food was not sufficient for the winter, and a re-supply would be needed. The Governor of the colony, John White, was selected to return to England to procure necessary supplies. Upon reaching England, Governor White found tensions with Spain so high that war seemed imminent. Expecting to need every ship in case of a conflict, the Queen would not allow any ships to depart. The expected war ended in August of 1588, when England defeated the Spanish Armada. Delayed by the preparations for war and the war itself, Governor White was unable to return to his colony for three years.

Upon his return in 1590, White found the colony deserted, but he discovered the pre-arranged message telling him where the colonists had relocated. A rather sudden and severe storm in the Atlantic prevented his going to that place. Due to the threat of great damage to their ships, Governor White's party was forced to sail away without locating the colonists. The records of this fifth and final voyage connected with Sir Walter Raleigh are the last recorded history of the colonists. In time this colony became known as the "Lost Colony".

There have been some bits and pieces of hard evidence recovered in the area where the colony was located, but there is a good deal of circumstantial evidence available that would suggest that the colonists survived and relocated.

There was a report in 1700 of Englishmen encountering a group of people who seemed to be of "mixed-breed", Indian and Caucasian. These mixed-breed people spoke English, lived in a civilized manner, and tilled the soil. It is the contention of the authors of this book that these mixed-breed people were descendants of the Lost Colony, and that they survive today as the Lumbee Indians who call Robeson County, North Carolina home.

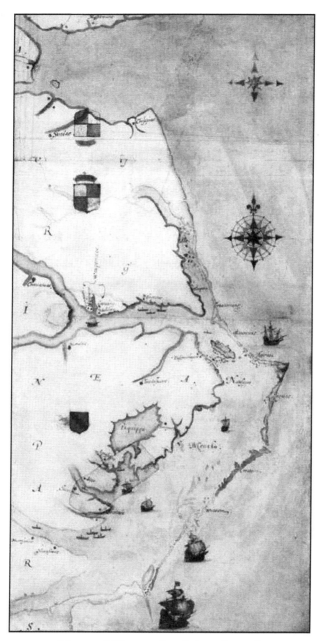

**Map of Roanoke Island and
Surrounding Areas**

Chapter 2

Significant Characters

Queen Elizabeth I (1533 – 1603)

Queen Elizabeth I was the daughter of Henry VIII and his second Queen, Anne Boleyn. Though both her parents were greatly disappointed by her sex, she was favored over Henry's elder daughter, Mary. Being sixteen years older than Elizabeth, Mary was old enough to be resentful of Elizabeth's position, and this caused friction between Henry's two daughters as long as Mary lived.

Elizabeth's childhood was lonely, and her position in the line of succession to the throne was questionable after her mother was beheaded by Henry VIII. She was an intelligent child, and her education was not neglected. She became fluent in six languages. As she matured, it was clear that in addition to intelligence, she also had inherited shrewdness and determination from her parents. These traits would serve her well throughout her life when she found herself in precarious situations.

Although Elizabeth presented an outward piety, her devotion to religion may have been a matter of convenience in her desire to maintain peace in England.

It was during her reign that the Church of England was firmly established as a blend of Protestantism and Catholicism, saving England from the ongoing religious wars that other countries experienced. Elizabeth did not tolerate anyone questioning her power, but she was wise enough to surround herself with good ministers to advise her. Under her reign, the arts flourished and foreign exploration paved the way for expanding trade and encouraging colonization, especially in America.

Elizabeth was well known for her elaborate fashion and her flirtatious relationships with numerous courtiers, but her devotion to England endeared her to the people. She chose never to marry, but considered herself "married" to the nation.

Old English Thatch-roofed Cottage

Sir Walter Raleigh (1552-1618)

Sir Walter Raleigh is most famous for establishing an English colony on Roanoke Island (North Carolina), where the first English child was born in America in 1587.

Raleigh was a man of many talents, a true Renaissance man. During his career he was a poet, a soldier, a courtier, a privateer, a navigator, a politician, an historian and explorer. His father was a gentleman of property in Devonshire with connections to many distinguished families, but he was of reduced estate. Sir Walter Raleigh was educated at Oxford. After serving in several military campaigns, he came to the attention of Queen Elizabeth I through connections at court and quickly became one of her favorites. When he first appeared at court, it is said that his court clothes made up the largest part of his estate.

He was a tall man of nearly six feet, with courtly manners and a quick wit. Raleigh was considered quite handsome, with curly brown hair and sharp but attractive features. He was flamboyant in dress and adorned himself with brightly colored jewels. All of these attributes won him a place close to the Queen's heart, and she made him wealthy by securing for him houses, lands, monopolies and grants. These gifts insured his position within the gentry class, but there were those at court who felt the Queen's largess was out of proportion to the value of his military service.

Lest anyone should think she was being unduly influenced by her current favorite, the Queen made a practice of having several "favorites" around her. Raleigh's prominence would last approximately six years. After that he seems to have lost his position, due in part to the Queen's habit of shuffling her favorites around to keep them off balance.

Raleigh's courtly manners and idealism may account for the tradition that he was such a gentleman that he threw his cloak over a puddle so Queen Elizabeth would not muddy her shoes. It seems appropriate that a cloak was part of his coat of arms. Raleigh's sense of adventure and far-sightedness fit well with his overwhelming desire for fortune and fame. He was energetic and hungry for new ideas. Some of his associates were the best scholars of the time. Notable among these were Thomas Harriot, a mathematician and scientist, and Richard Hakluyt, a writer and great promoter of expanding England's influence in the Atlantic with settlements in America. Both were influential in encouraging Raleigh's thirst for knowledge and adventure. Sir Richard Grenville was his cousin, and he was distantly related to Sir Francis Drake. Both men had a part in Raleigh's attempts at settlement of America.

Sir Walter Raleigh spelled his name in several different ways over his lifetime, but he never used the spelling which has become associated with him in modern histories. By the time Raleigh undertook voyages under his patent from Queen Elizabeth I, he seems to have settled on "Ralegh" as his choice.

Sir Walter Raleigh was the half-brother of Sir Humphrey Gilbert who had a patent from Queen Elizabeth to take possession of lands in North America. Gilbert had invested all of his money in unsuccessful expeditions, and his patent was going to run out in 1584. To prevent this from happening, Raleigh organized investors to fund an expedition to Newfoundland in 1583.

On the return voyage Gilbert perished. In March of 1584, Queen Elizabeth renewed Sir Humphrey Gilbert's patent with Raleigh, giving him and his heirs the rights to all lands they occupied in North America. In return, the crown was to receive twenty percent of all precious metals mined. So began Raleigh's attempt to plant a colony in America. After the return of the successful reconnaissance voyage of 1584, Queen Elizabeth was so pleased that she knighted him on January 6, 1585, and gave him permission to name the new territory "Virginia", in honor of the Virgin Queen.

As a result of Raleigh's charm, intelligence, and quick wit, he continued to enjoy the Queen's favor. In 1586, he received a large land grant in Ireland where he introduced potato and tobacco farming. In 1587, he received an additional land grant in England as a reward for his part in uncovering the "Babington" conspiracy, a plot to remove Queen Elizabeth and replace her with Mary, Queen of Scots. All of Raleigh's attempts at colonization in America proved unsuccessful. In 1589, he sold his rights to a company of merchants in return for a rent and twenty percent of any gold discovered. He continued in military service and in expeditions.

He was on an expedition at sea in 1592 when he was recalled by Queen Elizabeth upon her discovering that Raleigh had seduced one of her maids of honor. The Queen's maids of honor were not allowed to marry without her permission. If Raleigh had asked, it was unlikely she would have given her permission for one of her maids to marry one of her old favorites. Raleigh was imprisoned in the Tower, but later he married the maid.

When the expedition from which Raleigh was recalled returned with a valuable Portuguese ship, a dispute arose over division of the booty. Queen Elizabeth relented in her displeasure over Raleigh's behavior and released him from the Tower to see to the distribution of the booty. She took the bulk of it, but Raleigh received a sizeable sum.

Raleigh fell out of favor at court and retired to country life. Many at court were glad to be rid of Raleigh's brash ways and what they considered undue influence with the Queen. However, he was used to being involved with so many different interests that he was not happy being idle. He undertook another expedition and published an account of the voyage. He took part in the capture of Cadiz in 1596, and as a result was restored to favor at court.

When Queen Elizabeth died in 1603, Raleigh's real troubles began. When James I took the throne, he was already prejudiced against Raleigh. For years, Raleigh had been at odds with the Earl of Essex who was a compatriot of the new King.

In fact, as Captain of the Guard, Raleigh had presided over the execution of Essex for his rebellion. Besides this, King James was working quietly to obtain peace with Spain while Raleigh, a strong anti-Catholic, was ardent about continuing hostilities. James began to strip Raleigh of his titles and holdings, and eventually accused him of treason. In a trial that was wholly unfair, Raleigh was sentenced to death. However, he was not executed but sent to the Tower where he spent thirteen years. He occupied himself with writing, scientific experiments and trying to get the King to release him.

Finally, Raleigh came up with a fantastic plan. He promised the King that he could find a gold mine in Guiana without infringing on Spanish possessions. No one believed he could do it, but the King was desperate for money and willing to let Raleigh try. Not only was the expedition a disaster, but Raleigh's son and a number of Spaniards were killed. Furthermore, they found no gold! Spain put ever increasing pressure on King James to punish Raleigh, so upon his return to England the King had him arrested and executed under the old order.

Understanding Sir Walter Raleigh makes it easier to understand why his expeditions to America seemed poorly planned, inadequately supplied, and without backup plans. It also gives some indication of why he would not have been more persistent in searching for the colonists.

He appears to have been a man of many interests, but perhaps more interests than he could properly handle. In his own affairs, he managed to secure great fortunes, yet he was constantly finding himself short of funds. He seems to have enjoyed the excitement of being in the middle of things, but did not have the patience and skill to handle protracted ventures successfully.

The story of Raleigh's attempts at American colonization might have been different if Queen Elizabeth had granted patents based on proven skill and success rather than on charm and wit. Although Raleigh had distinguished himself in battle, particularly in Ireland, military skill was not consistent with planting a permanent colony. In fact, the skills used in Ireland of trying to subdue a population with force and harshness were the very skills that hindered colonization in America by alienating the native population.

In spite of his failure at colonization, Raleigh should be given credit for opening the way for future colonization. The lessons learned at Roanoke contributed to the success of the first permanent English settlement at Jamestown in 1607, in the location where the Roanoke colonists had intended to settle before they were forced to disembark on Roanoke Island.

Simon Fernando

Simon Fernando was an enigmatic character associated with the early explorations of North America and attempts to establish a permanent colony. He was Portuguese by birth, but he did not let that stop him from giving allegiance first to Spain and then to England. He was a ship pilot by training and became well known for his skill and experience in sailing to territories in the New World. Sailing the Atlantic Ocean, he discovered a passage into the sounds along the coast of North Carolina, and Port Fernando appears on early English maps of the area, apparently named in his honor.

He was born Simao Fernando on the island of Terceira in the Azores. During his lifetime, he was also known as Simon Fernandez and Simon Fernando.

Prior to sailing on Sir Walter Raleigh's voyages to the New World, Fernando had sailed for Raleigh's half-brother, Sir Humphrey Gilbert, when Gilbert was making voyages to Newfoundland and New England under a charter from Queen Elizabeth. Although Raleigh never sailed on a voyage under his own patent, he did sail under his half-brother's patent. It was on these voyages that Fernando and Raleigh formed an attachment that would later lead Raleigh to use Fernando as pilot of his voyages.

Fernando had the reputation of a skilled pilot, but his personal reputation was a questionable one. His activities were a bit murky, and he was known to be a pirate and a thief. He had a hatred of Spain, but it was probably while he was sailing for Spain that he became familiar with the West Indies, the coast of Florida and the east coast of America. Certainly the knowledge he gained of the Spanish trade routes benefitted him when he turned to piracy. When his piracy landed him in an English jail, with the Portuguese ambassador suggesting he should be hanged for piracy and murder, Fernando's fortunes took an unusual turn. Charges against him were eventually dropped with the intervention of the English Secretary of State, Sir Francis Walsingham, and the two men began a somewhat mysterious relationship.

Walsingham, who encouraged an English presence in the New World, was resented by many at court for his influence and power, and eventually there was talk of a conspiracy involving him and Fernando in attempting to thwart Raleigh's efforts at colonization.

Whether or not that was true, Fernando's curious behavior on Raleigh's voyage of 1587, when he deposited the colonists on Roanoke Island, changed the course of history and did nothing to dissuade historians from raising questions regarding his intentions.

Sir Walter Raleigh was confident enough of Fernando's abilities that he chose him as pilot on the voyages in 1584, 1585, and 1587. After completing those voyages, Fernando did not return to America. He disappeared from history after 1590, when he sailed to the Azores with an English fleet. It is assumed that he did not survive that voyage.

Sir Richard Grenville

Sir Richard Grenville was a British naval commander who is believed to have received his early military experience fighting the Turks under the Emperor Maximilian. During his career, he sat in parliament for Cornwall and was on the Parliamentary committee which recommended that Sir Walter Raleigh be granted a royal charter to found the first English colony in America. He was also High Sheriff of Cornwall, served as sheriff of Cork, Ireland, chased Spanish treasure ships as a privateer, engaged in the adventure of establishing England's presence in the New World, and fought against the Spanish Armada. He served as commander of the fleet for Sir Walter Raleigh's 1585 attempt to plant a settlement in America.

He was born about 1541, of an old Cornish family and was a cousin of Sir Walter Raleigh and Sir Francis Drake. He was a man of great pride and ambition with a rough, imperious nature. He delighted in astonishing people with his king-like behavior. In the colonizing venture of 1585, he was in a constant battle of wills with Master Ralph Lane who was in charge of the ground troops. He seemed to have a knack for irritating almost everyone. When they arrived at Roanoke, Grenville's harsh and arrogant attitude toward the Indians created tensions which would have repercussions for Lane and his men while they attempted to establish a colony after Grenville's departure.

Although there is some question as to Grenville's ability as a commander, no one questioned his bravery and willingness to fight against tremendous odds. These qualities were apparent when he was returning to England from Roanoke and spied a Spanish treasure ship ahead of him. Grenville had no small boat with which to board the Spanish ship, but he was determined to have her. He ordered his crew to quickly construct a makeshift boat by lashing together some ship's chests, in which he and a boarding party overtook the Spanish ship. No sooner had Grenville's party scrambled up the side of the Spanish ship than their "boat" fell apart and sank beneath them, but Grenville was successful in capturing the ship.

Perhaps his greatest adventure, memorialized in writing by Tennyson's "Revenge", occurred when he was serving as vice-admiral of a fleet of English ships in the Azores. His fleet was to waylay passing Spanish treasure ships, but they were suddenly surprised by the approach of a fleet of fifty-three Spanish ships.

The ships in the British fleet immediately put out to sea, but Grenville's ship was cut off. Grenville and his crew tried again and again to break the line of ships and fought for hours before he was mortally wounded. During the battle, his lone ship and crew of only one hundred able bodied sailors sunk or severely damaged four Spanish ships and killed or wounded one thousand Spanish sailors.

Grenville commanded his men to burn the ship rather than let the Spanish take it, but his men refused. Grenville was taken aboard a Spanish ship where the captain and crew were so impressed by his valor that he was treated by a doctor and shown great respect and kindness before he died of his wounds.

Ralph Lane

The birth and parentage of Ralph Lane are not certain. Some believe that he was born in Devon, England about 1530, and he may have been a cousin of Catherine Parr, the last wife of Henry VIII. In 1563, he began serving Queen Elizabeth as an officer of the royal household, collecting customs duties and enforcing the law. He served in Ireland and was knighted by Queen Elizabeth in 1593.

Lane is best remembered for his part in the unsuccessful attempt to establish an English colony in the New World in 1585. He sailed to Roanoke Island in Virginia on Sir Richard Grenville's ship, *Tiger*, and quarreled constantly on the voyage with the combative commander Grenville. Once at Roanoke Island, he was left with approximately one hundred men to explore the area and erect a stockade for defense.

Lane's explorations took him one hundred thirty miles into the country, but his suspicious nature and harshness toward the natives did not build the friendships necessary for a successful colony. At times he even resorted to kidnapping Indians to get information or supplies. In the end, he and his men abandoned the effort at colonization when Sir Francis Drake arrived and offered them passage back to England.

Lane continued to serve the Queen and died in 1603 from wounds received during an Irish rebellion.

Manteo and Wanchese

In 1584, the first ships sailed to America under Sir Walter Raleigh's patent to colonize the New World. After spending several weeks exploring the area of the Outer Banks of what is now North Carolina and enjoying a friendly welcome from the Indians, the explorers sailed back to England with two Indians, Manteo and Wanchese.

Little is known of these two Native Americans, but no doubt they were chosen because of their position of nobility among the Indians. The purpose of taking them back to England was to show them off to the court of Queen Elizabeth, but more importantly, Raleigh intended to decipher their language and interview them at length regarding their country and their people. Manteo and Wanchese were guests of Raleigh at his London residence, Durham House. He assigned Thomas Harriot, a brilliant scientist, the task of deciphering their Algonquian language. Harriot did this by using a phonetic alphabet of his own.

Manteo was the best student, and Harriot spent many days with him learning the Algonquian language and teaching Manteo English. Harriot also learned much about the Indian culture and life in the New World that would be of benefit to English settlers. He made note of the great awe with which the Native Americans viewed the advanced technology of the English.

They were particularly impressed with mathematical instruments such as compasses and spring clocks. Harriot reported that it was beyond their reason and comprehension to understand how such things could be made, and they considered them more the works of gods than men.

Manteo appeared to thrive under Harriot's attention and sense the great advantage of learning all he could about the English ways and even took to wearing English clothes. Wanchese on the other hand had little interest in learning and soon considered himself more a captive than a guest. Both Manteo and Wanchese returned to Roanoke Island with Sir Richard Grenville's fleet in 1585. Wanchese was glad to leave the English, but Manteo proved to be invaluable to the colonists in helping them survive their first winter in the New World. Manteo must have returned to England when the colony was abandoned in 1586, because he accompanied John White's colony from England to Roanoke Island in 1587.

It appears that Manteo was of the ruling family of the Croatan Indians, some of whom lived on Croatoan Island. Manteo had a close relationship with King Menatonon, who was ruler of the great nation, the Chawanooks. This would suggest that the Croatoan Indians were part of the friendly Chawanook nation. Manteo also had a friendly relationship with Wingina and his brother, Granganimeo, rulers of the Indians on Roanoke Island who extended friendship to the First Voyagers in 1584, as well as those of 1585.

The Croatan Indians lived in what is now Dare County, North Carolina in the Outer Banks area including the Alligator River, Croatan Sound, Hatteras Island and Roanoke Island.

Because Manteo learned the English language and had such an affinity for the English, he became invaluable to Sir Walter Raleigh's efforts to colonize America. He served as a guide, teacher and translator, as well as a mediator when relations became strained between the two cultures. He was instrumental in helping the colonists of 1585 survive and remained a trusted friend of the English. No doubt he was just as critical to the survival of the Lost Colony.

Manteo accepted the Christian religion, becoming the first American to become an Anglican Christian. Sir Walter Raleigh granted Manteo the title of Lord of Roanoke and Dasamonguepeuk, making him the first member of the English peerage in North America.

Nothing is known of Manteo's death. He returned to Roanoke Island with Governor John White's colony in 1587, which became known as the Lost Colony. His fate was entwined with that of the colonists.

Upon his return to Roanoke Island, Wanchese quickly became an enemy of the English. He aligned himself with chief Wingina, indicating that he was in the ruling family of the Roanoke Indians. Wingina eventually became hostile to the colonists, and after Wingina's death Wanchese assumed his position as the last known ruler of the Roanoke Indians.

colonists, and after Wingina's death Wanchese assumed his position as the last known ruler of the Roanoke Indians.

At the time of the English exploration, Dasamonguepeuk on the mainland was the chief town of the Roanoke Indians. They were one of the largest Carolina Algonquian tribes, possibly numbering over 5,000 throughout what is known today as eastern North Carolina. From the beginning, Wanchese was suspicious of the English and received little benefit from Harriot's tutoring and his association with the English.

Indians Fishing
(Engraving by Theodor de Bry from
a drawing by John White)

John White

Little is known of John White's early life, but he is best known for his remarkable watercolors of the New World, which gave a visual record of the flora and fauna, as well as the natives and their culture. White was on the voyages sent out by Sir Walter Raleigh in 1584, 1585, 1587 and 1590. His ability to create lifelike images, along with his journals and maps, served to influence the perception that Englishmen had of the New World. His drawings show great sensitivity and depth, especially those of the natives who were never posed but painted with a naturalistic style. Unfortunately, many of his watercolors, drawings and journals were lost in the hasty departure of the first colony from Roanoke in 1586. White's watercolors found a broad audience when they were engraved by Theodore de Bry and included in a volume entitled, **America.**

It is generally thought that John White was born in London between 1540 and 1550. There is no definite record of his education, though his journals are those of an educated man. It is likely that he apprenticed with a draftsman or artist to refine his skills. A John White appears in the 1580 membership records of a guild known as the Painters and Stainers Company of London. In addition to being an accomplished artist, he was also a skilled map maker and surveyor.

It is thought that White married between 1565 and 1570, and that he had at least one son and one daughter. His wife is presumed to have died prior to his voyages, but his daughter, Eleanor, and her husband, Ananias Dare, accompanied White when he was Governor of the 1587 voyage to Roanoke Island. It was his daughter who gave birth to Virginia Dare, the first white child born in America.

Almost nothing is known of John White after his unsuccessful attempt to locate the Lost Colony in 1590. He had been desperately concerned when he was unable to make a timely delivery of supplies to his colony and heartbroken when he was unable to locate them when he finally returned to Roanoke Island. Until his dying day, John White appeared convinced that his colonists had survived, though he was never able to find them. In a letter to Richard Hakluyt from his home at Newton in Kylmore County, Cork, Ireland, White commends *"the reliefe of my discomfortable company of planters in "Virginia", to the merciful help of the Almighty...."*

Chapter 3

Important People and Places

Master-Captain Philip Amadas: A member of the First Voyage in 1584, and captain of one of the two barks (ships) of that voyage.

Master-Captain Arthur Barlowe: A member of the First Voyage of 1584, and captain of one of the two barks (ships) of that voyage. He wrote the report of the First Voyage.

Master Simon Fernando (Fernandino): Pilot of one of the ships of the First Voyage of 1584, and Admiral of the fleet that transported members of the "Lost Colony" to America.

General Sir Richard Grenville: Commander of the fleet on the Second Voyage in 1585. He sailed on the ship *Tiger.*

Queen Elizabeth I: The Queen of England who granted Sir Walter Raleigh the right to attempt to establish colonies in North America in the area claimed by England.

Sir Walter Raleigh: The person to whom Queen Elizabeth granted the patent giving him the right to attempt the colonization of North America in the area claimed by England.

Master Ralph Lane: Member of the Second Voyage of 1585, who was in charge of the troops on land. He made explorations of the country and built a stockade. He wrote the report of the events of his explorations.

John White: Probably a member of the First Voyage of 1584. Member of the Second Voyage of 1585, and of the company of men who remained one year. He was Governor of the colony of the Fourth Voyage of 1587, and returned to England for supplies. He was unable to return to his colony until 1590, when he found the colony deserted. He wrote reports of the events of his voyages. He also painted many watercolors of the people, plants and animals of the New World.

Sir Francis Drake: Commander of the great fleet of ships which preyed upon the Spanish treasure ships returning from the New World. He carried the members of the Second Voyage back to England.

Ananias Dare: Son-in-law of John White, husband of Eleanor Dare, father of Virginia Dare.

Eleanor Dare: Daughter of John White, wife of Ananias Dare, mother of Virginia Dare.

Virginia Dare: First child of English parents born in America.

Manteo: Native American whose home was on Croatoan Island. He and his people, the Croatan Indians, were part of the nation of Chanooks. He visited England twice and became a devoted friend of the English. He was the first native to be christened and was given the title of Lord of Roanoke and Dasamonguepeuk in honor of his faithful service to the English.

Menatonon: King of the greatest province of Chawanook and a friend to the English. He was Manteo's King, and the reports of the Second Voyage refer to him as being impotent in his limbs. His main town was six day's journey from Roanoke.

Powhatan: King of a powerful confederation of Indian nations in present-day Virginia. He claimed that he slaughtered the members of the Lost Colony.

Wanchese: Native American who went to England with the return of the First Voyage. He spent a year in England, but upon his return to his native land he became a bitter enemy of the English.

Wingina: King of the country named Wingandacoa. He lived on Roanoke Island when the English first arrived, but moved to the mainland at a later time. He changed his name to Pemisapan upon the death of his brother Granganimeo.

Granganimeo: Brother of King Wingina who represented the king while he was injured and and unable to visit the English. He was the one who initially welcomed and entertained the members of the First Voyage. He was a wise man and a friend to the English.

Ensenore: King Wingina's aged father from whom he had inherited his authority. He was convinced that the English possessed powers greater than mere men and believed they were immortal. He was a faithful friend to the English and encouraged Wingina and others to show friendship to them.

Albemarle Sound: A large body of water inside the outer sand banks along the coast of North Carolina.

Cape Fear: The area of the Cape Fear River's confluence with the Atlantic Ocean. Sand bars extend some distance off shore, making navigation dangerous.

Chowanook: A large Indian nation located along the Chowan River. These Indians were friendly to the English.

Chowan River: A river in eastern North Carolina which flows from the north into the Albemarle Sound.

Cittie of Raleigh: The dwelling place of the colonists while living on Roanoke Island.

Chesapeake Bay: A large protected body of water with entrance from the Atlantic Ocean and extending north. It is located northward along the coast from Roanoke Island and was the intended destination of the Fourth Voyage. The native inhabitants of the area were known as Chesepeians.

Croatoan Island: An island lying south of Roanoke Island and bordering the Atlantic Ocean. This island was the home of Manteo and his people.

Croatoan Sound: A body of water lying between Roanoke Island and the mainland.

Cumberland County: A county located in southeastern North Carolina bordering Robeson County.

Cross Creek: An area of the present city of Fayetteville, N.C. In earlier years it was a village located near the Cape Fear River where two streams entered the river at different levels and flowed separately, forming a heart-shaped island before coming together downstream. Cross Creek was known by natives as Heart's Creek.

Dasamonguepeuk: An Indian village located on the mainland west of Roanoke and near the present city of Mann's Harbor.

Dismal Swamp: A great swamp lying between Albemarle Sound and Chesapeake Bay to the north, and from the Atlantic Ocean west to near the Chowan River.

Fayetteville: A city located in Cumberland County, N.C.

Hatorask: Earliest maps show this as an inlet located on the northern tip of the island then named Croatoan.

Hatteras Island: An outer sand bank island formerly known as Croatoan Island.

Hope Mills: A town located in Cumberland County, North Carolina.

Indian Wells: A site located on the northwest branch of the Cape Fear River about fifty miles upstream from Wilmington, North Carolina.

Jamestown: The site in the state of Virginia where the first permanent English settlement was located.

Lowerie or Lowery Trail: A great native trail which extended from the Neuse River to the Blue Ridge Mountains in North Carolina and eastern Tennessee.

Lumber River: The main river which flows through Robeson County, North Carolina where the Lumbee Indians were found.

Pamlico Sound: A large body of water lying between the outer sand banks and the mainland of North Carolina.

Pamlico River: A river which flows from the northeast into the Pamlico Sound.

Plymouth: A seaport city in the south of England used by Sir Walter Raleigh's ships.

Pomeiok: A native village located on Pamlico Sound

Portsmouth: A seaport city located on the southern shore of England and used by Sir Walter Raleigh's ships.

Okisko: King of several villages on the mainland bordering Albemarle Sound. His territory was the entire area along the shore of Albemarle Sound, stretching from the Atlantic Ocean to the Chowan River.

Roanoke River: A very long river which begins in the mountains of North Carolina and flows into Albemarle Sound.

Roanoke Sound: A body of water lying between Roanoke Island and the mainland.

Secotan: A native village located near Pamlico Sound and Pamlico River (also called Secota). Early maps also indicate Secotan was a large land area and perhaps an Indian nation. Probably in the area of present day Bath, N.C.

Weapomeiok: A native nation covering most of the area along the north shore of Albemarle Sound.

Wocokon (Wococon): An island of the outer sand banks, probably present day Ocracoke Island; also an inlet by the same name.

Chapter 4

Understanding the Colonists

What were the colonists of Roanoke's Lost Colony like? To understand the colonists, we must first view them in the setting of their mother country. In sixteenth century England, life was uncertain. The country had endured a history of rivalries between successive monarchs who often held radically different views which they enforced with vengeance. There was corruption and intrigue in the monarchy, the legal system and the church.

The church came under attack from both Catholic and Protestant monarchs, not only because of concerns over spiritual matters, but also because the church held great wealth and its ministers had strong influence. As the major countries of Europe constantly jockeyed for power and wealth, wars and rebellions went on between countries and within countries.

To add to the uncertainty of the times, King Henry VIII insisted on changing wives regularly, and finally changed his religion when the Pope would not sanction his adulterous lifestyle. Even change was uncertain. When Henry's daughter, Queen Mary I came to the throne, she set about undoing the changes her father and his successor Edward VI had made.

Mary was an ardent Catholic who was determined to rout out Protestantism from the country. In a three year period, she burned at the stake almost three hundred Protestants. Many fled the country to escape death.

It was a relief to most people when Queen Elizabeth I took the throne in 1559. She became head of the Church of England, and Protestantism was restored. Queen Elizabeth made it an act of treason to call her a heretic, as the Catholic Church did, or to deny that she was the lawful Queen. She imposed fines for not attending church and removed any clergymen refusing to recognize her as head of the church. Catholic priests were ordered out of the country if they did not want to face charges of treason. There continued to be Catholic rebellions in the north, and many rebels were hanged.

With such upheaval in the past, it is not surprising that Queen Elizabeth I set about to create a more cohesive society. She did this with a series of laws aimed at making sure everyone knew his place in the social order and obediently remained there. Monarchs were believed to be the representatives of God; therefore, the social ranks put in place by the Queen must be blessed by God. These laws so regulated society that they dictated not only the type and color of clothes each rank of society could wear, but also regulated how much money could be spent on such items as food, clothing and furniture. In this way, the monarchy could maintain a strict class structure and control behavior.

Such laws made it easy to identify a person's rank and privilege. This was convenient, since laws and punishments were applied according to rank.

Despite enforcing a strict class structure, Queen Elizabeth I was considered an intelligent and just sovereign. She was thought to be wise in her choice of advisors, and she purposely did not allow any one advisor to dominate her. In the same way she kept her courtiers uncertain of their status and vying for her favor. Her long reign of forty-five years is considered the English Renaissance.

Between the fifteenth and sixteenth century, there were great economic changes in England. The population increased dramatically, doubling between the reigns of Henry VIII and Elizabeth I. The standard of living dropped and unemployment rose. The poor became poorer. The average lifespan was under fifty years, and many children died in infancy or before reaching their teens. There was little medical knowledge, and most people relied on herbs and potions to treat common diseases such as diphtheria, measles, smallpox and typhus. Sanitation was poor, and the large cities were an especially filthy breeding ground for disease.

In the fifteenth century most of the country was in large tracks of land owned by the nobility or friends of the monarch. The land holdings were cultivated by large numbers of tenant farmers who had no hope of owning their own land or improving their station in life.

With most people employed in agriculture, workmen in towns were scarce so they were able to earn a substantial wage. By the mid-sixteenth century a change in land use brought yet another upheaval. The large land owners discovered that they could eliminate much of their workforce and make more money by switching from agriculture to raising sheep.

As the displaced farmers filled the towns and villages, wages dropped and inflation gripped the economy. With so many people out of work, begging became a problem across the country. Traditionally, the poor were given aid locally by almshouses supported by private legacies and by the monasteries. But Henry VIII had dissolved all of the monasteries, and there were not enough almshouses to provide for such large numbers of poor.

With these changes in the economy, Queen Elizabeth I and her advisors became concerned that such a large population of vagrants could lead to civil disorder. Over a period of years, a series of laws was passed aimed at giving some aid to the deserving poor and punishing those who broke the law. Punishments for non-deserving beggars ranged from running beggars out of town, merciless beatings, or even hanging them. Amputation was considered a minor punishment. At this period of English history, punishments were based on class and were violent and cruel.

In Tudor England, the people were divided ostensibly into several classes: nobility, gentry, merchant, yeoman, and laborers. However, in reality it seemed there were only two: one class consisted of nobility and gentry including Elizabeth's courtiers; the other class was everyone else.

This period of English history was marked by:

- Dramatic increase in population
- Change in the system of land use
- Displacement of large numbers of farmers
- Great increase in unemployment
- Increase in disease
- Rapid inflation
- Huge influx of beggars in villages and towns
- Increase in crime
- Lack of adequate support for the poor
- Religious intolerance and a desire to spread the Protestant faith

Considering the state of the social, economic, health, and financial situations in England in 1587, the hazards of a long voyage in a small ship to a strange, unsettled country probably seemed worth the risks. At least there a person would have the chance to make the life he wanted in a virgin land where society would need to be built from the ground up. It was the opportunity of a lifetime for those with vision and determination.

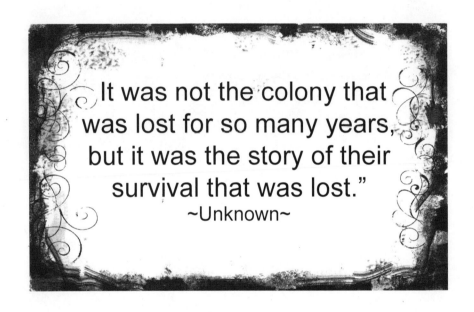

It was not the colony that
was lost for so many years,
but it was the story of their
survival that was lost."
~Unknown~

Chapter 5

Walk with Us - An Invitation

Walk with us through the narrow streets of our English towns and villages where we looked upon our friends and loved ones for the last time, burning their faces into our memories and their voices into our ears before we tearfully bade them farewell.

Walk with us in anticipation as we boarded the small sailing ships where we would be confined in crowed quarters for many weeks, sailing upon the waters of the Atlantic Ocean.

Walk with us who had never sailed before as we pressed into the stern of the ships, profound emotion rising in our hearts, for one last glimpse of our Mother Country.

Walk with us across the wooden decks as we faced into the wind beneath full sails, already relishing the smell of freedom.

Walk with us in the stifling air beneath deck where the smells of sickness, sweat and dankness caused us to question for just a minute if we had made a mistake in undertaking this voyage.

Walk with us to the stern of the ships after months at sea, eyes straining for any sign of the new land.

Walk with us as we came ashore in the country named Virginia and viewed the wind-swept sand dunes along the beach, the unfamiliar waters of the sounds, and the vast forests of the land that was to become our new home.

Walk with us as we were welcomed by the Native Americans who quickly became our trusted friends.

Walk with us as we gathered around our beloved Governor, John White, and requested with one voice that he return to England to procure much needed supplies.

Walk with us down to the Governor's ship where we bade him God's speed to return to us as soon as possible.

Walk with us in this beautiful new land as we faced an uncertain future and coped with the many challenges of our daily lives in strange surroundings.

Walk with us daily along the shoreline as we cast our eyes upon the Atlantic with the hope of sighting the sails of a ship bearing our Governor back to us with the supplies critical to our survival.

Walk with us as all hope of sighting a returning ship faded, as we turned our backs to the direction from whence we came and moved inland in order to fulfill our dreams and establish the first permanent English colony.

Walk with us and share our grief as we remembered our Mother Country, our loved ones and friends. Sense our anguish at the realization that we would likely never have news of our fellow countrymen.

Walk with us to understand the events that transpired so that you may appreciate our sacrifice.

Walk with us as we gave birth to a new nation, the nation you know as the United States of America.

Walk with us. May we share the future as one.

Glossary of Ships

Admiral (flagship): This was generally the largest and safest ship in the fleet; Commander of the fleet sailed on this ship.

Bark: small sailing vessel, propelled by oars and/or sails.

Consort: sailing vessel that generally accompanied another ship with an agreement to share any loot taken from another ship .

Flyboat: large ship of Dutch origin with high stern, broad beam and shallow draft.

Pinnace: small and light vessel, fast and maneuverable, sometimes used as message boat, highly regarded by the English for scouting coastal waters.

Chapter 6

Chronology of the Five Voyages Made Under the Patent of Sir Walter Raleigh

First Voyage: 1584

April 27: First Voyage sent to the New World with Captains Amadas and Barlowe

July 4: Ships arrived upon the coast of America

July 27: Ships reached the Outer Banks of North Carolina

Mid September: Ships arrived back in England with Indians, Manteo and Wanchese

Second Voyage: 1585-1586

April 19: Second Voyage to New World with Sir Richard Grenville in charge. Master Ralph Lane second in command

June 17: Grenville's fleet reached Croatoan Island on Outer Banks of North Carolina

July, late in the month: Grenville's fleet reached Roanoke Island

Aug. 25: Grenville sailed for England, leaving behind 100 colonists

1586:

June 10: Sir Francis Drake's fleet arrived at Port Fernando

June 16: Storm sunk 4 of Drake's ships

June 20: Drake returned to England with Lane and his colonists

Third Voyage: 1586

Sometime after Easter, a supply ship was sent by Sir Walter Raleigh and arrived immediately after the colony had departed; finding the colony deserted, the ship returned to England.

At the end of June, Grenville arrived at Roanoke Island with supplies. Finding the island deserted, he left 15 men behind to hold possession for England

Fourth Voyage: 1587

May 8: Fourth Voyage-Group of 118 men, women and children left Plymouth, England with Governor John White to establish a permanent colony in Virginia

July 22: Colonists stop at Roanoke Island to check on Grenville's 15 men. They found only the bones of one man. Pilot Simon Fernando forced them to remain at Roanoke Island instead of taking them to original destination of Chesapeake Bay

Aug. 13: Manteo christened and declared Lord of Roanoke and Dasamonguepeuk

Aug. 18: Eleanor Dare gave birth to Virginia Dare, first white child born in America

Aug. 27: Governor John White returned to England for supplies

Fifth Voyage: 1588-1590

Apr. 22: White sailed for Roanoke Island

May 22: After being robbed by privateers, White returned to England

May 28: Spanish ship discovered an apparently deserted English settlement on Roanoke Island

August: England defeated Spanish Armada

1590

Mar. 20: Fifth Voyage - John White sailed for Roanoke Island to find his colonists

Aug. 15: White found Roanoke Island deserted

Oct. 24: White reached Plymouth, England

Chapter 7

Significant Information
on the First Voyage – Comments

Even before setting foot in America, the first English explorers were predisposed to think it a paradise. As their ships drew nearer to land, those on board noticed "so sweet and so strong a smell as if we had been in the midst of some delicate garden abounding with all kinds of odoriferous flowers..." This was far different from anything they had experienced when approaching other lands. Being mid-summer, no doubt many flowers and trees were in bloom, but it may have been the scent from native fires burning sweet scented wood such as cedar or sassafras. In any case, the explorers were not disappointed in their expectations.

It is worth noting that on July 4, 1584, the first Englishmen "arrived upon the coast" of the land which would later become known as the United States of America. This moment was the birth of English civilization in America and was the foundation for the celebration of liberty the United States of America marked on July 4, 1776. So humbled were these men by the greatness of their venture that they felt it fitting to immediately offer thanks to God for a safe journey.

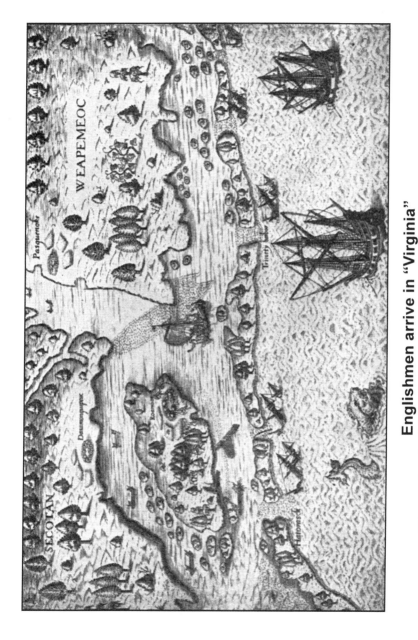

Englishmen arrive in "Virginia"
(Engraving by Theodor de Bry from a drawing by John White)

This First Voyage under Sir Walter Raleigh's patent from Queen Elizabeth I consisted of two small ships sailing from Plymouth, England on April 27, 1584.

Philip Amadas, a short-tempered man, commanded one ship and Arthur Barlowe commanded the other. Barlowe and Raleigh had fought together in Ireland. Although this was a reconnaissance voyage, there were some seventy-five soldiers and sailors on board.

It is probable that artist John White and Thomas Hariot, a mathematician and scientist, made the journey in order to collect specimens and make drawings of the natives and the plants and animals in the country. Hariot was also something of a linguist and would have been useful in deciphering the language of the Algonquian-speaking natives. The chief pilot was Simon Fernando, who had previously sailed with Sir Humphrey Gilbert, Raleigh's half-brother who first held a patent to explore unclaimed portions of North America.

The first recorded meeting in history of a Native American and an Englishman was a momentous occasion historians have given little attention. It was the first encounter between two vastly different cultures, one primitive and previously insulated and the other greatly advanced and expanding its sphere. The circumstances of this meeting made it most significant, as it was the beginning of the greatness of our nation of diverse cultures.

The first Native American encountered by the English did not run and hide. He stood watching without fear and waited for the Englishmen to row ashore. (It is likely these natives had been told by the people of Secotan of white men who had washed ashore more than twenty-six years before and been entertained by the natives until the white men departed.) He spoke to them in his language, which they did not understand, and he willingly went with them on board their ships to have a look around.

The Englishmen responded as guests arriving in a new country, offering him gifts and a meal. The native then departed and went to his own boat where he began to fish. He divided his catch into two portions and laid one on shore before each of the two ships, the indication being that he was making a gift to each ship.

The native exhibited exceptional bravery. He had never seen any human with white skin nor such clothes as they wore. He had never seen a watercraft except a canoe, yet he boldly went aboard each ship. He displayed no fear of being taken prisoner or any other misfortune. Surely, the English were surprised and delighted to have such a positive introduction to the Native Americans.

The next day, a native they came to know as Granganimeo, who was the Indian King's brother, appeared with about fifty handsome and mannerly men. They laid a mat upon the ground where the king's brother sat at one end and four of his companions at the other end. When the Englishmen came ashore with their weapons, still no one showed any fear. Granganimeo motioned for them to join him sitting on the mat. He proceeded to make a speech and gestures of friendship which the Englishmen understood to mean "we were all one".

During this meeting the Englishmen learned an important piece of information. The King himself, Wingina, whose country was known as Ossomocomuck (Wingandacoa), was not present because he had been severely wounded during a fight with the King of the adjoining country. He survived his wounds and was recovering at their main town, six days journey away.

The importance of this information is two-fold. The Englishmen now knew that this new land was not under the control of just one King, and it was divided into different "countries". Also, there were hostilities between the Kings. As chief of the Roanokes, Wingina ruled the towns of Secotan and Dasamonguepeuk on the mainland, as well a village on the northern part of Roanoke Island.

After this encounter, the King's brother later returned to the English ships with his family, still showing no fear. He wanted to barter for hatchets, axes and knives in exchange for animal skins. He was particularly anxious to obtain the swords and armor of the Englishmen, offering a box of pearls in exchange. Although reports of the voyage tend to portray the Indians as almost childlike and mild-mannered, Granganimeo understood the advantage these items would give him in battles with other groups of Indians.

Attire of Roanoke Indians
(Engraving by Theodore de Bry from
a drawing by John White)

The Englishmen refused the pearls, because they did not want to give the impression that they valued pearls until they were able to determine where the Indians got them. One purpose of colonization was to enrich England with valuable goods found in the New World and one box of pearls, without knowing the source, was not going to do that.

In the course of bartering, Granganimeo made it clear that when he or his nobles were present, all bartering would be done with them, not with any of the other Indians. The Indians had a clearly defined hierarchy and were devoted to their royalty.

The King's brother proved to be a man of his word and very generous, sending the best foods to the ships every day. As they developed their relationship with the natives, the Englishmen were able to observe that they wore jewelry made of copper or gold, and they used very good dyes.

All of these were the types of commodities that would make America a source of wealth to England. The Englishmen were also able to observe the Indians' method of planting and the great fertility of the soil.

Traveling upon the waterways, the colonists came to the island of Roanoke, where they observed a small village with houses made of cedar. Cedar would be of interest to the Englishmen for export to England. Queen Elizabeth was determined to make England the major maritime nation at a time when ships were made of wood, and the fine, strong wood required for shipbuilding was becoming scarce in England. Here the wife of the King's brother warmly welcomed them and sent men into the water to bare the Englishmen ashore, others to secure their boat, and others to bring their oars inside so they would not be stolen. This is an important detail that will have consequence in a future voyage. Apparently, either stealing was common among the Indians, or it was simply that the oars were an irresistible prize. There are cultures to this day where stealing is not considered a moral issue, but simply an opportunity that presents itself.

The King's brother was not present, but his wife made every effort to show all courtesy to the Englishmen, going so far as to have their clothes washed and dried before presenting them a bountiful table. In their description of the bounty was another important detail. They described drinking water flavored with "ginger in it, and black cinnamon, and sometimes sassafras and divers other wholesome and medicinable herbs and trees".

At this time in history, sassafras was quite expensive and considered a cure-all, highly valued in the treatment of syphilis which was spreading across Europe. The Englishmen would also have interest in any medicinal herbs, since an English housewife had to serve as doctor to her family and usually cultivated herbs for that purpose. New types of medicinal herbs would be valuable, and cinnamon and ginger would be important spices for export.

This gathering convinced the Englishmen that the Indians were "most gentle, loving and faithful, devoid of all guile and treason, and such as live after the manner of the golden age. The people only care how to defend themselves from the cold in their short winter, and to feed themselves with such meat as the soil affords…"

It is easy to see how they formed this opinion. While they were eating, several men returned from hunting with bows and arrows. When the Englishmen saw them, they started to

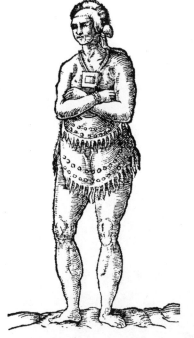

Roanoke Chief

reach for their weapons, but Granganimeo's wife immediately sent others out to take away their bows and arrows, break them and beat the men away. Clearly, she did not intend the Englishmen to feel any uneasiness. She was disappointed when the Englishmen would not stay ashore for the night, but sent them to their boat with food for supper. The Englishmen took their boat some distance from shore, giving the impression they did not feel safe.

The wife of the King's brother was so distressed that she sent a group of men and women to sit on shore all night keeping watch, and sent mats to the boat to protect the Englishmen from rain. Though they were entreated to stay the night in the Indians' homes, the Englishmen thought it best, since they were so few, not to take a chance of endangering their mission. However, they stated that they believed they had no cause to doubt the Indians, "a more kind and loving people cannot be found in all the world, as far as we have hitherto had trial…"

In spite of Barlowe's glowing words about the friendliness of the Indians, the existing drought conditions had reduced their stores of food so that some of the Indians seemed uncertain about the arrival of the Englishmen. Philip Amadas and Simon Fernando took one of the ships to the vicinity of Albermarle Sound where they encountered Indians who were not so friendly.

The English also noted that the Indians would "tremble thereat for the very fear and strangeness of the same" whenever an Englishman fired even one of their small guns. The Indians possessed only bows with cane arrows tipped with a sharp shell or tooth of a fish. Their swords were of hardened wood.

These weapons would pierce naked skin, but were no match for the weapons and armor of the Englishmen. The Indians also used wooden breastplates and made a sort of club from an animal's sharp horn. When the Indians went into battle, they carried an idol for counsel. In recent times, the Indians had been engaged in bloody battles over civil dissensions and many had been killed.

The two Indians the Englishmen later took back to England said that a peace agreement had been made between the warring Indian Kings, but the Secotans still held a grudge for a particularly treacherous act of King Pemisapan. As a result, the Secotans were continually trying to get the English to do a surprise attack on Pemisapan's town where they promised the English would find great spoils. The English suspected the Secotans were trying to get them to exact revenge.

The Englishmen reported that there were many other islands with towns and villages and the same on the mainland. They had quickly discovered that what they first thought to be the continent was one of many islands separated from the continent by a sea.

They reported a river called Cipo where pearls were to be found. They also discovered that two other kings, Pooneno and Menatonon, controlled areas along the river and that they were in league with King Wingina.

Surprisingly, the Indians told them that twenty six years earlier, a ship was cast away not far from the southernmost town of King Wingina's territory, and a number of white people survived and were rescued by the Indians of Secotan.

The white people remained for ten days on the uninhabited island of Wocokon, when the Indians helped them fasten two of their boats together. The white people put masts on the boats and used their shirts for sails. They gathered what food the island provided and after being there three weeks, set sail. Not long after, the boats were found cast away on an adjoining island, but the Secotan Indians, the only ones ever to have seen these white people, never saw them again. Arthur Barlowe recounts that this was surely true, because the Indians showed such awe upon seeing the Englishmen.

The Englishmen on this First Voyage felt they had explored and reported as much as possible in the time they had, but hoped to have other opportunities to do more exploring. When they departed for their return voyage to England, arriving in mid-September, they brought with them two "savages" who wished to see England, Manteo, the son of the Croatoans' chief, and Wanchese, a Roanoke Indian closely associated with Wingina.

No doubt these two ambassadors from America wanted to see the land of the Englishmen and perhaps find out the source of their power and if it could be obtained by the Indians. It should be noted that the use of the term "savage" in the context of these voyages of exploration and colonization did not have the same meaning as it does today. From the description of the Native Americans in the report of this First Voyage, no one could believe that the Englishmen viewed these people as wild, uncivilized, brutal, and lacking manners. To the Englishmen, the term "savage" applied to those not of the Christian faith.

Certainly, with its great strength England would have prevailed in conquest, but the overall welcoming reception received during this first visit shaped the Englishmen's opinion that the natives could be won over by friendship and respect. This initial fascination with the natives and admiration for their country was lost on the leaders of the Second Voyage.

Virginia Indian Chiefs
(Engraving by Theodor de Bry from
drawing by John White)

Chapter 8

Significant Information
on the Second Voyage

From Ralph Lane's report to Sir Walter Raleigh and other documents, we know that the Second Voyage in April 1585, was a large contingent of seven ships of various sizes and well supplied. Men with experience fighting England's wars were in charge, and the venture took on a decidedly military nature. It is noteworthy that in his writing Lane did not preface the year with the common phrase, "in the year of our redemption", found in the report of the First Voyage. This was an early indication that the mission originally stated by Queen Elizabeth in Raleigh's patent had changed. This change in point of view was reinforced when upon safe arrival at Roanoke, Lane made no report of any thanks being offered to God for His bringing them safely to their destination. Such a prayer upon arrival was the first order of business on the previous voyage. No thought seems to have been given to the Almighty until a year later when the Englishmen feared for their lives, and the venture ended in a dangerous and hasty departure. Even then it was not a member of the Second Voyage who invoked God, but Sir Francis Drake, who came to their rescue.

The only one on the voyage who seemed concerned with spreading Christianity in accordance with Raleigh's patent was Thomas Hariot. He wrote that at every opportunity he proclaimed to the Indians the doctrine of salvation through Christ.

Sir Richard Grenville, Raleigh's cousin, was in command of the fleet (the General) and was Captain of Queen Elizabeth's flagship (or Admiral), *Tiger*.

The pilot of this lead ship was Simon Fernando, who was on the First Voyage. Colonel Ralph Lane, who received much experience fighting in Ireland, was Master of the troops on the voyage. Philip Amadas and Arthur Barlowe, who captained the two ships of the First Voyage, were also on this voyage.

Amadas was chosen as admiral of the fleet and second in command to Grenville. All of these men were either friends of Sir Walter Raleigh, or in some way related to him. While Grenville and Lane undoubtedly possessed skills valuable in wars and insurrections, it does make one wonder if Sir Walter Raleigh gave much thought as to their qualifications for creating friendly and mutually beneficial relations with the Indians and for establishing a colony among them. If the purpose of the voyage was conquest, these men were well suited to the job, but probably not the best choice as ambassadors and diplomats. It is interesting to speculate what influence their personalities had on the success of the colony.

The bull-headed Grenville did not get along well with Lane, and there was open bitterness between them. In fact, Lane made it clear at the end of the venture that he never again wanted to serve with Grenville. There were other officers and gentlemen on the voyage who were often at odds with Grenville due to his reportedly tyrannical nature.

Four ships of the fleet belonged to Raleigh: *Dorothy*, *Roebuck* (John Clarke, Captain), and two pinnaces which were smaller vessels often used in shallow waters or rivers where larger ships could not sail. Two other ships completed the fleet, *Elizabeth* (Thomas Cavendish, Captain) and *Lion* (George Raymond, Captain).

The voyagers included a number of gentlemen in addition to the captains and assistants, who were expected to provide counsel and direction for the voyage. John White, a distinguished watercolor painter, who would also serve as surveyor, and Thomas Hariot, mathematician and scientist, were brought along to make a pictorial record of the natives and the land, as well as to study their culture and language. The ships carried approximately three hundred men (some sources say six hundred), including those men who would colonize Roanoke. The colonists included some men with practical skills such as a surgeon and carpenters, but some were likely impressed from the streets of cities and towns in England. It was a common practice to impress men when needed, and no one cared where they were to be found.

Manteo and Wanchese, the two Indians who accompanied the First Voyagers on their return to England, were now coming home after being tutored in the English language by Hariot while they taught him the Algonquian language. Manteo seems to have had an inquiring mind which caused him to throw himself into learning the language and absorbing as much as he could of the culture and religion of the English. He was comfortable wearing English-style clothes and perceived the benefits of becoming more like the English. On the other hand, Wanchese did not embrace his experience in England with enthusiasm. His personality appears to have been more brooding and stand-offish. He was not comfortable around the English, and he was anxious to return home. Manteo's interest in all things English endeared him to his benefactors, while Wanchese's solitary nature kept him distant and jealous of their attentions to Manteo. The difference between the two would have consequences later on for the colonists. While in England, it is likely that Manteo and Wanchese were presented at court in an effort to raise funds for this voyage.

Those on board the ships probably included both sailors to man the ships and soldiers to participate in the privateering expected to help pay for the voyage. Because of the risky nature of the voyages, Queen Elizabeth I was not interested in financing them, but she was determined to establish England's presence in America.

Elizabeth viewed privateering as a useful way to provide financial backing for colonizing, as well as a way to enrich England's treasury. While she did not officially condone the practice of privateering, she found it convenient to turn a blind eye to it. Her stance had a significant impact on the actual nature of the voyages, as the lure of Spanish treasure ships was always paramount in the minds of the voyagers.

There is some reason to believe there was coordination between this voyage, under command of Grenville, and another much larger one at the same time under the command of Sir Francis Drake. The logic to this connection is that Raleigh's fleet, under the command of Grenville, would establish a base at Roanoke from which Drake, a well-known and skillful privateer, and other English captains could hunt Spanish ships in the Caribbean.

During the first month of the voyage, Grenville's ships followed the southern route established by Columbus to the Canaries, the Antilles and Hispaniola. Unfortunately, Grenville's ship, the *Tiger*, piloted by Simon Fernando, was separated from the fleet in a severe storm near Portugal. The pinnace accompanying the *Tiger* sunk in the storm. By a prearranged plan, in case of separation they were to meet in Puerto Rico. So Grenville sailed on, stopping at Cotesa near St. John Island, where everyone went ashore to refresh themselves.

On May 12th, the *Tiger* was anchored in the Bay of Moskito on the south side of Puerto Rico. Grenville knew he was in what was considered Spanish territory, but apparently he felt he needed to replace the lost pinnace in order to navigate the sounds and rivers around Roanoke.

While waiting for the other ships to arrive, Grenville and most of the party went ashore and constructed a fort with a river on one side and woods on two sides, taking into consideration that an attack by the Spanish could come from land or sea. Ralph Lane would have been the most likely person to oversee the construction of the fort.

They set up a forge for making nails and felled trees as far as three miles inland to build a new pinnance. At that time in history, there were two techniques used to construct small vessels. The method most likely employed by Grenville's men used green wood with the boards nailed without caulking and overlapped on the sides of the boat. Although this method produced a boat that created more turbulence in the water and a rougher ride, its ease of construction made it preferable under the circumstances, to the method requiring cured wood, matched planks and caulking.

The island had been inhabited by the Spanish for many years, but Lane noted that although the Spanish observed what the English were doing, they offered no resistance.

Another ship of the fleet, *Elizabeth*, arrived on May19th, after being separated in the storm off the Bay of Portugal and sailing three thousand miles to join the *Tiger*.

On the 22nd, the Spanish came to complain about the English constructing a fort in their territory, but Grenville's military training compelled him to meet them with a superior force. The Spanish were solicitous at first, but demanded to know why the English were there at all and what right they had to build a fort.

The English assured them they wanted only to get water and provisions, either in a friendly manner or by force. The Spanish agreed to help them. Their acquiescence did not comfort Grenville, and he felt that all haste should be used in completing construction of the pinnace in order to depart as soon as possible.

On the 23rd, they completed construction of the pinnace and launched it. Some of the English rode up into the country to collect supplies promised by the Spanish. The Spanish did not appear. In retaliation for this disrespect, the English set the woods ablaze before returning to burn their own fort. Then everyone went on board the ships to get ready to depart. During their stay on the island, John White made detailed drawings of their fort and the local plants and animals.

Grenville had grown tired of waiting for the rest of the fleet to arrive, so the two ships and the newly constructed pinnace sailed on the 29th. They came upon a Spanish frigate and took it when the Spanish abandoned ship upon seeing the English. The very next morning they took another frigate containing valuable freight and important Spaniards. The next day, Ralph Lane took one of the Spanish frigates to Roxo Bay in St. John Island, where he had been told by one of the Spanish pilots that he would find salt.

Here Lane and twenty men took over one of the salt hills and loaded their ship under the eye of the Spanish, who once again did not interfere. Lane rejoined the fleet in St. Germans Bay. The following day the fleet arrived at Hispaniola where they ransomed the captured Spaniards.

On the 3rd of June, the Governor of Isabella sent word that he would visit the English in a few days. When the governor and his party came, they had already been informed of the brave and gallant Englishmen. The English did all they could to impress the governor and his party by providing a grand banquet. The Spanish provided saddled horses for everyone to participate in sporting entertainments. The English and Spanish exchanged gifts. It is possible that some of the gifts presented by the English were part of the booty on the captured Spanish ships. The following day the English used the gifts presented them by the Spanish to barter with local merchants for horses, goats, bulls, pigs, sheep, sugar, ginger, pearls, tobacco, etc. They departed on the 7th, hunted seals on the 8th, and arrived at Isle of Caycos on the 9th, where they had been told by a Portugese they would find salt ponds. The information was false.

After seeing how lightly fortified these Spanish islands were, it seems most likely that Grenville would have conveyed this information back to England. It was just the kind of information that would be valuable to privateers such as Sir Francis Drake.

Stopping at Guanima and Cyguateo, they reached what Lane calls "Florida" on the 20th of June, and on the 23rd were in danger of wrecking on "the Cape of Fear".

One must remember that the entire eastern part of America from present-day Florida to Canada had been named

"Florida" by the Spanish and appears as such on maps of the period. It is more probable that the ships reached Cape Fear in what is now North Carolina. That area has dangerous shoals and the sea floor is littered with wrecked ships.

When Lane writes that they came to anchor on the 24th of June in a harbor filled with fish, he is probably referring to Cape Lookout in what is now North Carolina. Cape Lookout is a day's sail from Cape Fear and has a deep harbor. Lane made no mention of putting out small boats to check for depth, as he would have done had he been entering an inlet. Apparently, it was clear to him that the harbor where they made their first landing on the 24th was a deep water harbor. Since their next anchorage was just two days later in Wocokon, it would be highly unlikely that they could have sailed such a distance in so short a time from any harbor in present-day Florida. The Spanish already had a military presence in the area of what is now the state of Florida, including a strong fort at St. Augustine, so it doesn't seem reasonable that the English would have risked a battle by anchoring there.

On the 26th, they anchored at Wocokon, a barrier island of the Outer Banks of North Carolina. On the 29th, they weighed anchor to bring the *Tiger* into the harbor. The ship was grounded due to the lack of skill of the ship's pilot, Simon Fernando. He was on the First Voyage and had also sailed for Raleigh's half-brother, Sir Humphrey Gilbert. They feared the ship would be lost, but finally they were able to free it (and later make repairs so that it was again seaworthy). By that time, the hold was awash, ruining most of the provisions they had brought to sustain them for a year.

They were able to salvage only enough provisions for twenty days. Lane did not report it, but it may be presumed that the animals they had collected in the Caribbean either fell from the ship when it went aground, or were thrown overboard to lighten it. Grenville and Lane must have recognized the implications of this disaster for the survival of the colony, and perhaps that explains why Grenville eventually chose to leave behind only one-hundred colonists out of the three-hundred who made the voyage. The optimum number of colonists suggested in the early planning stages for this voyage was eight-hundred. The difficulties of securing enough ships, supplies and men whittled that number down to three-hundred colonists by the time they sailed, and it seems almost inconceivable that Grenville expected success in colonizing the new continent with only one-hundred men. They would need reinforcements.

On July 3rd, they sent word of their arrival at Wocokon to the Indian King Wingina at Roanoke.

On July 6th, John Arundell and Manteo went ashore on the mainland. Captain Aubry and Captain Boniten went to Croatoan, where they found two of their men, plus thirty others, left there by Captain George Raymond twenty days before. Captain Raymond was in command of a ship of the fleet, *Lyon*, which after being separated in a storm from the flagship, had made its way alone to Virginia. It has been assumed that when Captain Raymond found no other ships at Roanoke, he deposited these men on Croatoan Island and quickly sailed away to go privateering. His plan probably was to return before sailing for England. Indiactions are that the ships *Roebuck* and *Dorothy* and a pinnace eventually made it to the Outer Banks. On July 8, Captain Aubry and Captain Boniten returned to Wocokon with their two men.

On July 11, Grenville, Ralph Lane, several captains, and a contingent of men, as well as artist, John White, sailed from Wocokon to the mainland with supplies for a week so that they could explore the interior. They discovered the towns of Pomeiok, Aquascogoc and Secotan in the territory of King Wingina known as Ossomocomuck, as well as Lake Paquique. At every point the Indians received them with friendship.

On the 15th, they were entertained by the Indians at Secotan. John White made detailed drawings of what he saw in these villages and a map of the area. On the 16th, Grenville sent Philip Amadas, referred to as "the admiral" during this voyage, on a mission to Aquascogoc to retrieve a silver cup which they believed had been stolen by a native. When the cup was not returned, the English burned the natives' corn and their town, causing them to flee.

Indians making a canoe
(Engraving by Theodor de Bry from a
drawing by John White)

Lane gives little explanation of this incident and reports it with amazing detachment. This heavy handed reaction by the English would have future repercussions. It is particularly troubling because this behavior was at odds with the official policy of Raleigh's charter "to live together in Christian peace". One of the supposed purposes of exploration of new lands was to extend the Protestant faith. Why would these experienced military men bring violence to a rather minor incident and risk ruining their chance to make Christians of the natives? A silver cup would seem a small price to pay for the souls of so many.

Perhaps the English were feeling especially superior after the deferential treatment from the Spanish in the Caribbean. The silver cup may well have been a prize possession taken from one of the Spanish ships. There could be many explanations, but here we see the military nature of the expedition exposed. This was an overreaction one might expect from men used to resorting to force to establish their control as conquerors, but they were supposed to be "colonists", not invaders. In spite of the romanticized reports of the First Voyage, England surely expected to become the ruler of this country, or Spain would. The possibility should be considered that Lane and Grenville may have been instructed to quickly establish a fear of the mighty English so there would be less possibility of resistance from the natives. If that were true, the missing cup takes on a more sinister aspect.

It may have been a ruse created to justify a display of what the natives could expect if they crossed the English. That would explain why these men were already acting as rulers. In any case, the English stepped off on the wrong foot right from the start.

The English reached their fleet anchored at Wocokon on the 18th and on the 21st sailed for Hatorask, not arriving until the 27th, possibly due to bad weather. On the 29th, King Wingina's brother, Granganimeo, came aboard the admiral ship with Manteo.

On August 2nd, the admiral ship sailed to Weapomeiok. On the 5th, Master Arundell sailed for England and on the 25th, Grenville aboard the *Tiger* set sail for England, promising to return by Easter the following spring.

About the 31st, the *Tiger* captured a richly loaded Spanish ship which was separated from the annual convoy of treasure ships returning to Spain. Grenville stayed on the captured ship and in foul weather on the 10th of September lost sight of the *Tiger*.

On October 6th, the *Tiger* landed at Falmouth and on the 18th, Grenville landed at Plymouth aboard the captured ship. So richly laden was this prize ship that all who had invested in the 1585 voyage were handsomely rewarded.

Approximately one hundred men were left at Roanoke under the leadership of Master Ralph Lane, expecting Grenville to send supplies and additional colonists by Easter the following spring. When the last ship departed, Lane was left with only a few small boats for use in shallow waters.

Ralph Lane's Letter To Richard Hakluyt (1585)
(An Extract)

Ralph Lane praised the mainland as having very fertile soil and abounding with fine trees, grapes, herbs for medicine, flax, corn, and cane for making sugar. Lane and his men could not guess at the vastness of the land, but Lane mentioned that there were many towns and people. Significantly, he reported that it was such a healthy climate that not one of his men had been sick since their arrival. This lack of pollution, which was also reported on the First Voyage, seemed to have been one of the most impressive things about the new land. The environment was quite different from the filth and disease that was common in London and other parts of England. At a time when medical care was almost non-existent for the common man, this would have been an important observation.

The territory was described as having all of value that could be found in any other place, including oil, rosin, pitch, frankincense, and currants, but because the natives were not as advanced as the English they did not know how to put these products to the best use. Copper was mentioned as an item the natives valued highly.

Lane commented that if there were only horses and wine available, it would be the best place in Christendom. For the English, the world was divided into two realms: Christians, and all others who did not accept the Christian God and were referred to as heathen or "savage".

From the glowing reports of the love, friendship, and courtesy extended by the natives, we know that the Englishmen did not consider the natives to be savages in the sense of being brutal or uncivilized. They simply were not Christians.

"Indians sitting at meate"
(Engraving by Theodor de Bry from a drawing by John White)

Ralph Lane's Report to Sir Walter Raleigh
An Account of Settlets in Virginia (1585-1586)

Lane began by stating that his report would be in two parts. First, he will describe the mainland as far as the size of his party and their resources would allow them to discover. The second part will detail the reasons they felt compelled to leave with Sir Francis Drake's fleet when it arrived, bringing them provisions and boats to leave with them for their stay. He mentioned that the boats were carried away by foul weather. Then Lane added that he will also explain a conspiracy of "Pemisapan with the savages of the main to have cut us off..."

The Englishmen of the First Voyage were very impressed by the culture of the American Indians and their kind and loving ways. They were men who seemed to admire and respect the natives. Their time with the natives was short (six weeks), and perhaps they exaggerated the qualities they wished to see in the natives. Their report must have given Sir Walter Raleigh the impression that the natives would be just as welcoming and accommodating to a large group of over one-hundred men of various backgrounds, coming to settle in their country, as they had been to the courteous group who visited only briefly on the First Voyage.

Considering the number of ships involved in the Second Voyage, the good quantity of supplies they carried, and the additional supplies they collected in the Caribbean, as well as the advance plan to resupply the colonists, it would appear that the Second Voyage had a strong chance of planting a permanent colony. However, they encountered difficulties from the start, beginning with their fleet getting separated on the voyage.

During the year the members of the Second Voyage remained as colonists, problems and hostilities arose. Lane did not enumerate the reasons, but it is not difficult to conclude from what he did say that most likely the large group of Englishmen who had lost their provisions became a burden to the Indians. Unfortunately, there were conflicting aims among the voyagers. Colonization was supposed to have been the major concern, but most of the men left behind were soldiers and adventurers more concerned with quickly finding gold or silver to make them rich. When that didn't happen, they became disgruntled. They were not colonists and had absolutely no skill or desire to produce or procure their own food. Once their supplies ran out, they made constant demands on the natives to supply them food, when the natives did only subsistence farming to provide for their own needs. In addition, the men may have been too involved with the native women.

There is another possible reason for the change in the relationship of the Indians and the Englishmen. Between the First and Second Voyage, the Indians witnessed a total eclipse of the sun.

Soon after Grenville's ships arrived on the Second Voyage, the Indians watched a comet move slowly across the sky. They considered these as significant signs. When an often fatal illness spread quickly among their people, the Indians considered all of these things related. The initial awe and respect the natives showed the English may have turned to fear and mistrust.

Lane failed to find a good deep water harbor necessary for resupplying a colony. In fact, the treacherous waters off the North Carolina coast and the maze of small islands to confuse ship pilots convinced Lane they were not in a suitable location for a colony. He had also failed to find gold and silver or a "passage to the south sea".

In the end, a venture which should have established a firm foothold for the English in America, with the Indians as their friends and supporters, turned out to do little more than alienate the natives and make them fearful of the English. One "treasure" of this venture turned out to be the beautifully detailed drawings and watercolors of John White which depicted the Indian villages, dress, agriculture, and way of life. He also made sketches of the flora and fauna, as well as drawing a detailed map. White's drawings are now in the British Museum. The other "treasure" was Thomas Hariot's observations of the country, "A Briefe and True Report of Virginia", which he published in 1588.

Typical Indian Village
(Engraving by Theodor de Bry from a
drawing by John White)

The First Part Declaring the Particulars
of the Country of "Virginia"

Lane reported that his party explored from their settlement on Roanoke Island to the south, north, northwest and west. The farthest south they went was Secotan, about eighty miles distant. Their exploration south was through a sound in one boat with oars that was suited to the shallow water. The boat could carry no more than fifteen men with their provisions for seven days. Because winter was coming on and they were such a small party, they decided to leave further exploration to the south for another time.

Northward they went as far as the Chesepians, about one hundred and thirty miles. Here, too, the water was shallow. The Chesepians lived fifteen miles inland in what Lane described as a fertile land abounding with trees, wildlife, and seafood, as well as having an excellent climate. He made note of sassafras and walnut trees.

Lane found there were several kings called Weroances, in other fertile countries adjoining the area: Mandoages, Tripanics, and Apossians, who all came to see the English. This indicated that the Indians already had a political division of the land and a social order in place.

To the northwest they went as far as Chawanook, about one hundred thirty miles from Roanoke. They passed through a broad sound of fresh water good for shipping and navigation.

The towns along the waterside were Passaquenoke, The Woman's Towne, Chepanoc, Weapomeiok, Muscamunge, and Metoackwen. These towns were under the jurisdiction of the King of Weapomeiok, called Okisco. From Muscamunge, they went by river into the jurisdiction of Chawanook and followed the river to a good high land on the left bank with a town the English called The Blind Town, but called Ohanoak by the natives. The town had a large corn field.

Chawanook was the greatest province on the river, able to put seven hundred fighting men in the field, in addition to other men from the province. The King of Chawanook province was Menatonon, a man with weak limbs, but a serious and wise man who was well acquainted with the force and commodities of all the lands around him.

The king was a valuable source of information to Lane. It is very telling that Lane described obtaining this information, *"when I had him prisoner with me, for two days that we were together".* One must wonder if all of this information the king gave Lane was out of friendship or in order to send him off in another direction where the king would be rid of Lane. He described the island fortress of another king which lay in a bay near the sea surrounded by deep water. (The King Menatonon referred to was Powhatan and the island fortress was the later site of the Jamestown settlement.) This king took great quantities of pearls from the sea and had so many that he used them to decorate his home and the clothing of his people.

The King of Chawanook told Lane that this particular king had visited him two years before and sold him pearls of inferior quality, but at a great price. The king gave a string of black pearls to Lane, but they were lost with some of his other goods when Lane came aboard Sir Frances Drake's fleet. The King of Chawanook explained that the black pearls were from shallow water, but the other king had great numbers of large, round, white pearls which came from very deep water. Menatonon seemed to indicate to Lane that the other king had contact with other white men who bought all of his pearls so that he would give none but black pearls to the natives. These white men wore clothes like the English, but Lane does not speculate on who these white men might be. However, some consideration should be given to the fact that there were reports from the Jamestown colony of Indians with "gray eyes" seen in the area north of Roanoke. This contact with other white men raises the question as to whether these Indians with gray eyes were descendants of the other white men mentioned by the King of Chawanook, or descendants of members of the Lost Colony as many believe. There is the possibility these white men were Spanish. Exactly who they were is a question that remains unanswered.

The King of Chawanook promised to give Lane guides to take him to this king at the sea, but warned him to take many men and much food because this king would not welcome any strangers in his territory or any fishing for pearls. This king commanded a great many men who were good fighters.

Lane then explained in a rather self-serving way that had Grenville sent supplies and boats on time, he would have sent men in a ship to this island and would have taken other boats up to the head of the Chowanook River, with two-hundred men and the best guides Menatonon could provide.

Apparently, Lane had taken Menatonon and his favorite son prisoner as a means of securing their help. It is difficult to understand why Lane would have made prisoners of the king and his son when the purpose of his being in America was to build friendly relations with the Indians and to establish a cooperation with them that would be beneficial to both in developing the resources of the land. Making prisoners of the natives, no matter how well they were treated, did not fit with those purposes. Perhaps Lane's experience in putting down rebellions in Ireland predisposed him to wield the same heavy hand with the American natives. This seems more the response of a military man than an ambassador. Lane indicated that he released King Menatonon after he paid a ransom but sent his son on to Roanoke, still a prisoner.

Lane's intention was to continue his explorations with a company of men, hoping to find the Moratoks or the Mangoaks to supply them food. Lane's plan from this area to the sea was to build defensive works approximately two days apart and leave men stationed at each one. A main fort for defense of the harbor and shipping would be raised at the sea. Lane intended to remove his whole company from Roanoke with its inferior harbor to the new deep water harbor.

He then described a somewhat convoluted conspiracy of how Pemisapan (Wingina), who had changed his name from Wingina upon the death of his brother Granganimeo, pretending to be his friend, convinced Lane that the mainland Indians were planning to wipe out his group so that Lane needed to act preemptively. Pemisapan feigned friendship even further by hinting that the Indians Lane would attack knew where there were mineral mines, which certainly peaked Lane's interest. At the same time Pemisapan convinced the Indians that Lane was coming to attack them.

When Lane came to Chawanook, he did indeed find a large gathering of natives, but Lane reported that his unexpected appearance gave him the upper hand. Lane said Menatonon told him the whole thing was cooked up by Pemisapan, who kept telling the Indians that Lane's purpose was to wipe them out and so they were ready to respond in the same manner.

Apparently, the faulty news that Lane's men were hostile caused the people along the river, even the Moratoks whom they previously had been in league with, to flee their towns and take all of their provisions with them. This put Lane's party in danger of starving, apparently part of Pemisapan's plan, and Lane put the decision to his men to return the way they came or go forward with the exploration. Lane mentioned that he felt Indians traveling with them had betrayed them. While Lane was busy laying the blame of betrayal on the different

Indians, he seemed unaware that his report was revealing a great deal about his inability to understand the natives and their relationships. He seemed fooled at every turn.

Unanimously, the men agreed to go forward, but in the end were reduced to eating their two dogs and boiled sassafras leaves. They determined to push on to the sound where they felt they would be able to find fish to eat.

Lane wanted to find the Mangoaks and take some prisoner, since they were rumored to know where there were mineral (copper) mines on the Moratoc River. Apparently, everyone in the country knew about the mines, including Skiko, son of the King of Chawanook who had earlier been prisoner of the Mangoaks. Lane said he wanted to get some of this copper from the Mangoaks to have it assayed.

Things did not go as planned. As they traveled the river, they heard some savages calling in the evening. Lane thought it was a welcome, but Manteo, who was with them, told him the savages meant to fight. At once the Indians shot arrows, hurting no one, and running away when the boats landed. The party spent the night ashore and in the morning agreed to head back toward the sound due to the lack of food. They made their journey with nothing to eat until they got to the sound. The Indians all fled, but they did get fish to eat from their traps. The next day they arrived back at Roanoke.

This conspiracy which Lane related in detail was possibly an exaggeration. He may have believed it, or he may have used it simply to explain away some of the shortcomings of his exploration. He seemed ill equipped to build friendly alliances with the Indians and often appeared almost paranoid.

We know from Lane's own reports that from the beginning, his men did not plant corn, did not set fish traps, did not learn to build or repair the fish traps, and depended almost entirely on the generosity of the Indians to provide them with food. So the easiest way for the Indians to be rid of the Englishmen would not have been with an elaborate war conspiracy and chance of injury, but simply to have done nothing and let them starve.

Lane assured Sir Walter Raleigh that it was most worthwhile to pursue exploration of the mainland and mentioned that he had already established fortifications along the way. He bemoaned the fact that he would have done more exploration if he had been better supplied. Then he stated that the lack of supplies which deterred him might have been the purposes of God at work unknown to him.

Cooking Fish
(Engraving by Theodor de Bry from a
drawing by John White)

Chapter 9

Significant Information on the Third Voyage

Richard Hakluyt, the historian and geographer who wrote the report of Lane's company of colonists, painted quite a heroic picture of the men finally despairing of resupply and resigning themselves to spending the rest of their lives on Roanoke Island. He described how they immediately set about planting enough crops to last them for two years, but seemed to miss the point that anyone going as a "colonist" should have taken this action from the start. After all, the purpose of the venture was to plant a permanent, self-sufficient colony. Certainly the reports of the First Voyage made it clear that the soil was fertile enough to produce abundant crops and that there was sufficient naturally growing food to supplement the diet of those who would come to settle the land.

As Hakluyt explained the colonists' confused departure when Sir Francis Drake unexpectedly arrived and agreed to take them back to England, he surprisingly switched tone and stated that all of the chaos was caused by God as a punishment for the cruelty and outrageous acts they had committed against the Indians.

Although the supply ships Ralph Lane expected before Easter did not arrive on time, Raleigh had not forgotten about the Colony on Roanoke. Delayed by the political situation in

England, including the English support of the fighting against the Spanish in Flanders (Netherlands), Raleigh provisioned a supply ship at this own expense and sent it to Roanoke after Easter.

The ship arrived almost immediately after the colonists had deserted Roanoke in favor of returning to England with Sir Francis Drake's Fleet.

Those arriving on the supply ship were surprised to find the encampment empty. They made an effort to locate the colonists, but had no way of knowing that Sir Francis Drake had made an impromptu stop at the colony and had carried away everyone, except three men who were left behind in the frantic departure. Just prior to Drake's arrival, Lane had sent these men out into the countryside in search of any food they might find to sustain the colonists. They must have been quite startled and alarmed when they returned and found their entire party had vanished. If Lane felt the hostile attitude of the Indians was threatening to a company of over one hundred, imagine the fear three lone men must have felt.

Finding no colonists, the supply ship returned to England with its cargo. There is no mention that the three men left behind by Lane were ever sighted by those on the supply ship. As a matter of fact, they were never seen again by white men. Later there were differing stories told by the Indians about their fate. Some claimed the three were murdered by the natives, but others said at least one escaped.

About two weeks later, Sir Richard Grenville arrived at Roanoke with a small fleet of ships full of the promised provisions and some additional colonists. He was surprised when he found neither the other supply ship, nor any sign of the colonists he had left behind the previous year. Obviously, neither Raleigh nor Grenville had received news before these supply ships left England that Lane and his men had abandoned the settlement. When Raleigh did learn of it, he was furious with Lane.

Grenville made a search for the colonists, but found no one and apparently could get no information from the Indians. Grenville did not want a colony which he planted to fail, so he left behind a group of fifteen men with provisions for two years. They were to hold the territory for England. Grenville departed with his fleet, privateering on his way back to England.

Grenville must have been completely ignorant of how badly the situation had deteriorated since he left the colony, or surely he would not have expected such a small party to be sufficient. With no other information than what he witnessed at the settlement, he should have concluded that something extraordinary must have happened to cause all of the colonists to desert the island. Even if Lane and his men had gone on an exploration mission, they would have left a small contingent of men behind to "hold the fort" and keep watch for the expected supply ships. Grenville's seeming indifference There is no way he could have believed that such a small to what would become of the fifteen men he left behind may be a commentary on the regard for human life at this period in history. group of men would be able to secure the colony if the Spanish discovered it and decided to take it. Perhaps Grenville's well-known arrogance clouded his reason. The fifteen men he left behind joined the growing number of those "missing" in the attempts to plant a permanent colony in America. When the voyage of 1587 arrived at Roanoke, those colonists discovered the bones of at least one of the men Grenville left behind. The fate of the others remains uncertain.

Typical Style of 16th Century
English Fort

Chapter 10

Significant Information on the Fourth Voyage

Sir Walter Raleigh was upset with Ralph Lane for abandoning the colony on Roanoke no matter how he tried to justify himself. This was an expensive venture to simply abandon, plus it could not have enhanced Raleigh's position at court, or with his financial backers. A number of Raleigh's previous associates in his colonizing ventures seemed to have lost interest. In spite of this set back and the fact that his attention may have been diverted to other areas by the political situation in England, he was still willing to make another attempt at a permanent settlement in Virginia. He surely must have been anxious to go himself and directly supervise the next attempt at settlement, but the Queen was not willing to be deprived of his company.

This time Raleigh gave due consideration to the reports he had received regarding the explorations of the Chesapeake Bay and decided that area was much better suited to deep-water navigation than Roanoke. Also, the Indians of that area appeared friendly and had not been alienated by Englishmen. There he planned to establish his "Cittie of Raleigh", instead of on Roanoke Island. Raleigh also changed his voyagers, recruiting men with wives and families.

They had a personal stake in the success of the venture, either investing in it, or at least responsible for their own equipment and supplies. As an added incentive to attract colonists, Raleigh promised five-hundred acres of land in Virginia to the head of each household making the voyage.

While preparations were underway for the proposed voyage of one hundred and fifty colonists, twelve "assistants" were given the task of recruiting these colonists. Naturally, this produced a passenger list of several groups related by blood or the bonds of friendship. These close connections likely proved crucial in the survival of the colony.

Once again, Raleigh chose Simon Fernando to pilot the flagship, *Lion*, even though he had not shown the greatest skill on the Second Voyage, grounding a ship, spoiling their supplies, and putting the survival of that colony in danger. Fernando was not well thought of by his sailors, who called him "the swine". It is difficult to understand why Raleigh would risk so much on a pilot who had been a major factor in the failure of the last colony.

To lead this mission, Raleigh chose artist, John White, who was not a military man. White brought along his pregnant daughter, Eleanor Dare, and her husband Ananias Dare, as well as over one hundred others, including family groups. Among the colonists were men with valuable skills such as a basket maker, a husbandman, a tailor, and probably a doctor.

This seemed like a group well-suited to establishing a permanent colony which would be a self-sufficient agricultural community. They were in effect a small village being transported to Virginia.

On May 8, 1587, 118 colonists sailed from England with a fleet of three ships. The original number of one hundred and fifty colonists had been reduced by financial and other problems. Two Indians, Manteo and Towaye, who had been in England and were now returning home, were also on board.

Simon Fernando was pilot of the flagship, *Lion*, while Edward Spicer was in command of a fly-boat and Edward Stafford commanded a pinnace. This was Fernando's third trip to "Virginia", while White, Stafford and a few others of the men had served under Lane on the previous voyage and were returning for the second time. They took the West Indies route, rather than sailing directly to Virginia.

On May 16, Fernando abandoned the fly-boat in the Bay of Portugal. This was not a good start, and John White surely was not happy. The mixed purposes of the principals, one set on establishing a permanent settlement and the other determined to engage in privateering, undermined the success of the venture. One purpose of taking the West Indies route was for the chance of privateering, and Fernando was not about to let problems with the fly-boat hold him back.

The fly-boat would have to follow as best it could. Fernando stopped at Santa Cruz on May 22, and put all of the "planters" ashore. For someone who was familiar with the Caribbean, Fernando seemed to have chosen the worst possible place to stop. Not only was there no water fit to drink, but many of the planters ate an unfamiliar native fruit that caused their mouths and tongues to swell so that they could not speak. Others fell ill from drinking stagnant water, which was all they could find. Fernando had assured them that this was an uninhabited island, but that proved untrue. They remained there until May 25.

Fernando sent Captain Stafford in the pinnace to an island called Beake near St. John, where he was to find plenty of fresh water. The planters departed Santa Cruz and arrived at Cottea on May 27, where they found the pinnace. The next day they went to Musketos Bay at St. John and spent three days taking on fresh water. In the process they managed to consume more beer than they replaced with water.

On July 1, they departed Musketos Bay, leaving behind two Irishmen. No explanation was given for leaving without these men. Writer Dale Keiger in an article entitled "Rethinking Roanoke" (Johns Hopkins Magazine) reviews the work of anthropologist Lee Miller, who states that the Irishman, Darby Glande, gave a sworn deposition that he did not desert the ship, but was told to leave.

He alerted the Spanish to the destination of the ship, and the coordinates he gave almost exactly matched Roanoke, not Chesapeake Bay. Had Fernando already decided that he was not going to the Chesapeake Bay as instructed by Raleigh? Perhaps the Irishmen knew too much and talked too freely to suit Fernando.

Sailing on to Rosse Bay, Fernando instructed the colonists to gather all of the sacks they could find. He promised they would find salt there to add to their supply. However, when they arrived at the bay, Fernando confessed he wasn't sure it was the same place he remembered, and it was too dangerous to take the pinnace into the bay. He even staged a little "crisis" to make sure he got his way, cursing and swearing at the helmsman to "bear up hard!" to convince them it was impossible to go ashore. So they left without salt.

Fernando's curious behavior was not over yet. When they came to St. John the next day, John White wanted to go ashore at St. Germans Bay to gather plants such as orange trees, which he knew would grow well in "Virginia". Fernando would not agree, but said he would land instead at Hispaniola where he had a friend named Alanson, who could help them find what they needed. He promised to allow White and his assistants to go ashore in the pinnace, where Alanson would help them get cattle in addition to any plants they would have found at St. Germans Bay.

They sailed along the coast of Hispaniola all of the next day, but Fernando made no preparation for the pinnace to go ashore. They continued sailing along the coast until John White was sure they were past the point where Alanson supposedly lived. White asked Fernando if he planned to stop, but Fernando came up with some wild story that Sir Walter Raleigh told him that the King of Spain had recalled Alanson to Spain. Fernando said they were already past the place to land, and he believed his friend was dead anyway, so there was no use to stop at all. John White must have been troubled greatly by the strange behavior of the pilot, but Fernando did not have to answer to White.

On July 6, they reached Caycos Island where Fernando promised there were two salt ponds. Like all of his promises, this proved untrue. While he relaxed on shore, the planters searched for salt ponds to no avail, caught some birds and many swans. The ships left the next morning and the planters hoped the next land they saw would be "Virginia".

So far the trip through the West Indies had been a waste of time, and Fernando seemed curiously unfamiliar with an area he was supposed to know well. This odd behavior has caused some to speculate that he was in league with persons in Queen Elizabeth's court who did not want to see Sir Walter Raleigh's venture succeed.

The court swirled with intrigues of one kind or another, and Raleigh's ardent disposition favoring an immediate and heavy handed move against the Spanish did not set well with those in a position to benefit from a more protracted approach. Walsingham, the Queen's Secretary of State, heads the list of those who were jealous of Raleigh's meteoric rise in the Queen's favor and his captivating influence on her. There was a connection between Walsingham and Fernando that seems a little peculiar. Fernando was once arrested for piracy, a crime punishable by death, but his release was arranged by Walsingham. What the relationship between the Secretary of State and a rather scandalous navigator could have been is not known. If there were not a conspiracy, Fernandos' behavior seems inexplicable for a supposedly skilled and highly regarded navigator.

About July 16, they finally came in sight of Virginia. Fernando anchored for two or three days off what he thought was Croatoan Island before he decided he was mistaken. This was the pilot who was experienced sailing in this area and who was so well-known for his skill that a part of the coast had been named in his honor (Port Fernandino). Could he really have been so confused? He weighed anchor and proceeded along the coast, where during the night he narrowly missed running aground at the Cape of Fear. It was only the careful watchfulness of Captain Stafford which prevented a disaster. White writes that the near disaster was due to *"the carelessness and ignorance of our master"*.

Knowing from previous experience that this area was particularly dangerous for ships and that careful watchfulness was required, one must question why Fernando decided to weigh anchor and sail at night rather than wait until morning.

On July 22, they arrived at Hatorask where the ship and pinnace anchored. With all of Fernando's dawdling in the West Indies, the trip had taken twice as long as it should have and put the planters in Virginia too late in the season to plant crops to sustain them through the winter. John White and forty of his men went on board the pinnace so they could sail up to Roanoke to check on the fifteen men left the year before by Sir Richard Grenville. They planned to find out from these men how they were faring and about the state of affairs with the Indians. They would then return to the ship to proceed on to Chesapeake Bay, according to Sir Walter Raleigh's written instructions, to settle there and construct a fort. However, as soon as White and his men were settled in the pinnace, Fernando instructed the sailors not to return any of the planters (colonists) to the ship, except for White and one or two others whom he would approve. Fernando excused his action by saying it was so far into the summer (the best season for privateering) that he refused to take the time to deliver them to Chesapeake Bay before he left. This was one of those decisions which changed the course of American history, but it is given little attention by historians. Since all of the sailors were under the command of Fernando, White must have seen no point in arguing just then and sailed on to Roanoke.

Fernando was disobeying written orders from Sir Walter Raleigh, and if a strong military man had been governor instead of White, he would likely have called Fernando to account. It does not appear that Fernando was punished at all, even when White wrote a letter stating that he believed Fernando had sabotaged the venture.

Curiously, in spite of his supposed rush to depart, Fernando hung around until almost the end of August before he sailed for England. The planters must have been seething to see Fernando sitting aboard his ship out of their reach, while he could have been delivering them to the Chesapeake Bay. It was bad enough when he stranded them on Roanoke, but as events unfolded day by day, their anxiety must have increased tremendously. No one in England knew where they were. Any English ships desiring to stop to check on them on the way back to England would go to Chesapeake Bay, not Roanoke Island. When Fernando finally set sail, he did not return to prime hunting territory in the West Indies, but instead sailed directly to England by way of the Azores. This was just one more bit of odd behavior.

When White and his party went ashore at sunset on Roanoke Island, they did not find any sign of the fifteen men. All they found were the bones of one of the men who had apparently been killed by the Indians.

The next day, White and some of his company walked to the north end of the island where Ralph Lane had built his fort and several dwelling houses. What they found was that the fort was razed, but the houses were still standing, overgrown with pumpkins, and the deer grazing in them.

They left without hope of ever seeing the fifteen men who had been left there, but John White decided that they should immediately begin to repair the houses still standing and build other cottages needed to house everyone. Some historians have criticized White for not being more forceful with Fernando by demanding that he carry out Sir Walter Raleigh's instructions to take the colonists to the Chesapeake Bay. It has been suggested that his compliance even makes it appear that he and Fernando had already agreed to this change of plans.

However, White seemed at odds with Fernando throughout the voyage and not his ally. John White was an observer and artist, not a soldier. From what is known of his participation in the Second Voyage, he appeared to be a man of compassion and gentleness. These were qualities well suited to building friendship with the Indians and securing their assistance in establishing a successful colony. If he did not appear forceful with Fernando, perhaps it was because he knew he could not win in a confrontation, and he saw no point in frightening the planters by letting them think this change put them or the mission in danger.

To everyone's great joy and relief, Captain Spicer's fly-boat, carrying the rest of the planters, arrived safely at Hatorask on July 25. White wrote that this did not please Fernando, who deliberately abandoned the fly-boat in the Bay of Portugal, hoping that its master, Edward Spicer, who had never been to "Virginia", would not be able to find it, or that a lone ship would likely fall prey to all of the Spanish men-of-war in that area. White then added, *"...but God disappointed his wicked pretenses."*

On July 28, the newly arrived planters got a brutal introduction to their new home. One of John White's twelve assistants, George Howe, strayed away from the group to catch crabs. Before entering the shallow water, he had removed most of his clothes and left his weapons on shore. Hostile Indians, who had come over to Roanoke to hunt the plentiful deer or to spy on the English, ambushed him. Hidden among the reeds, the Indians shot him with sixteen arrows before he had any chance to defend himself. They also used their wooden swords on him and then bashed in his head before they fled across the water to the mainland.

On July 30, Master Stafford, who likely had previous experience with the Indians when he served under Lane on the Second Voyage, and twenty men sailed to the island of Croatoan with Manteo. The report of the voyage contained these words, *"... Master Stafford and twenty of our men passed by water to the island of Croatoan, with Manteo, who had his mother and many of his kindred dwelling in that island..."*.

This statement indicated that others of Manteo's tribe must have been in other locations on the mainland. That would be consistent with John White's drawings which showed the Indian villages as consisting of between eight and twelve dwellings, which would not have been adequate for all of Manteo's tribe. During their visit to Croatoan, they hoped to get some news of the fate of the fifteen men who were missing and also to determine the current attitude of the natives toward the English. It was their hope to renew their friendship with the natives, since it would be vital to the survival of the colony.

The Roanoke Indians had tried to turn the Croatoans against the English and convince them the English were their enemy. When Stafford's group came ashore, at first the natives appeared to want to fight, but when the English marched toward them with their guns the natives turned and ran. Since Manteo had taken to wearing English-style clothing, they probably did not recognize him. But as soon as Manteo called out to them in their own language, they ran back, embracing Manteo and the English and begging them not to take any of their corn because they had so little. Obviously, the Indians remembered the way Ralph Lane's men from the Second Voyage had demanded to have food supplied to them. The country was in the midst of one of the worst droughts in its history, and food was scarce. The English assured them that they did not intend to take any of their food and only desired to renew old friendships and be as loving to one another as they had been when first they met.

This seemed to relieve any apprehension the Indians had, and they invited the English to come to their village where they entertained them as was their custom.

Village of Pomeioc
(Engraving by Theodor de Bry from a drawing by John White)
Used Courtesy Univ. of VA

However, old fears were not completely forgotten. The Indians requested they be given some badge or token so that the English could clearly recognize them as their friends whenever they met them outside their village. They explained that they were afraid of being attacked again as Ralph Lane had done when he did not recognize them as friends. They even showed the English one of their group who was lame from that experience. The Indians said they knew in that instance that they had been mistaken for Wingina's men (who had turned hostile to the English), so they did not hold the English responsible.

The Croatoan Indians were surprisingly forgiving and seemed more fearful than angry. The English must have seen that they would have to work to restore trust and friendship with the Indians if they hoped to make their colony a success. To that end, on August 1, the English asked the people of Croatoan to carry a message of goodwill to the Kings of Secotan, Aquascogoc, and Pomeiok, expressing to them their willingness to forget past grievances on both sides and become friends again. The Indians agreed to carry this message and promised to have the kings or governors of these people to come with them within seven days to meet with John White, or to bring their answer.

The Indians further told the English that Howe had been killed by a remnant of Wingina's men who lived at Dasamonguepeuk.

They also told them that Wanchese, the Indian who had gone to England along with Manteo but who later turned against them, was in the company of Wingina's men.

They learned from the Indians the fate of the missing fifteen men. They said men from Secotan, Aquascogoc, and Dasamonguepeuk hid behind trees to observe near the houses where these men lived without much thought of danger. When they saw that only eleven men were there, two of the savages came forward, calling to the Englishmen in a friendly manner and asking that two of them should come unarmed to talk with the Indians. As the savages appeared unarmed and friendly, two Englishmen went out to meet them. As soon as they got close, one of the savages embraced one of the Englishmen while the other savage uncovered his wooden sword and hit him on the head, killing him.

Then twenty-eight savages hiding behind the trees rushed in and chased the other Englishmen back to the house where all of the Englishmen took refuge. The savages then set the house on fire, whereupon the Englishmen grabbed the first weapons at hand and ran outside to fight. The savages had the advantage of tree cover and nimbleness while they skirmished for an hour. An Englishman and an Indian were killed and some Englishmen injured before they ran to a boat on the water side and fled to Hatorask. When they had gone only a quarter of a mile, they saw four of their men returning from a creek where they had been to find oysters.

They quickly took these men into the boat and eventually landed on a little island near the entrance to the harbor to Hatorask. The Englishmen stayed there only briefly before they left, but the Indians didn't know where they went. After obtaining this information, Stafford and his men returned to their fleet at Hatorask.

When the appointed time passed without the appearance of the mainland kings or any message from them, John White decided to take matters into his own hands. On August 8, John White, Captain Stafford, Manteo, and twenty-four men crossed the water to the place Manteo directed them. Early in the morning of August 9, before it was yet light they crept up on their enemy (the Roanokes) and found them sitting around fires. White's men immediately rushed forward, but the natives fled into nearby reeds to escape. In the commotion, one native was shot before the Englishmen discovered they were mistaken. Sitting around the fire, the natives were so similarly dressed that they all appeared to be men, but fortunately before any more damage was done the Englishmen saw that one was a woman with a baby on her back.

About the same time, one of the natives rushed forward calling Captain Stafford by name. These were their friends, the Croatoans, who explained that all of those involved in killing George Howe had fled immediately afterwards, and the Croatoans had simply come over to collect the corn, peas, tobacco, and pumpkins left behind before the birds and deer could spoil them. It is not certain what tokens the Englishmen had given the Croatoans to distinguish them from hostile Indians in just this kind of situation, but apparently they were not visible in the darkness.

Realizing their mistake, the Englishmen helped the Indians gather up everything that was left and took them to Roanoke. Manteo was a little disturbed by what had happened, but he showed his loyalty to the English by telling the Indians that the whole thing was more or less their own fault, because if they had convinced the kings to come to the meeting called by White, this incident never would have happened.

On August 13, by pre-arrangement with Sir Walter Raleigh, Manteo was christened in Roanoke, becoming the first Native American to accept Christianity and to be christened. He was also made Lord of Roanoke and Dasamonguepeuk, the territory of the hostile deceased King, Wingina, as a reward for his faithful service. Conferring this honor upon Manteo was a wise move, as it served to rout any lingering hostile followers of the dead Wingina from the area. It was also the first instance of the English conferring a title of nobility upon a Native American.

The christening of Manteo seems to be the only overt religious aspect of Raleigh's efforts at colonization. Clearly, the leaders of the First Voyage and John White on this voyage were men of faith, but it doesn't appear that Raleigh made any effort to recruit devout christians for his colony.

Despite the fact that one stated purpose of colonization was to spread the Protestant faith, Raleigh seemed more or less indifferent to that purpose. Many question whether Raleigh was a strong Christian at all, or if he simply followed the form of religion as required to advance at court. It is fair to question whether Raleigh was the best man for establishing colonies with a religious charge.

Eleanor Dare, daughter of John White, gave birth to a baby girl on August 18. Eleanor's husband Ananias Dare was one of the assistants of the colony. Since this baby was the first Christian born in "Virginia", she was christened Virginia the following Sunday. John White surely would have painted or at least sketched a portrait of his daughter with her infant, the first child born in America to English parents, but there remains no evidence of that. It is unfortunate that so many of his papers, painting and drawings were destroyed by accident or by plunder, so that our knowledge of this settlement is not as great as it might have been.

By this time, the planters' possessions and supplies had been removed from the ships, and wood and fresh water had been brought on board. Whatever work was required to prepare the ships to sail was being completed. The planters prepared letters and remembrances to send back to England. Just as the *Lion* and the fly-boat were about ready to sail, a northeast storm struck with such fury that Fernando was forced to put out to sea with his ship. The ship was beaten about for six days before he could bring it back into the harbor. The planters were especially concerned, since most of the best sailors had been left on shore.

John White and his assistants were having trouble deciding which two assistants they should send back to England to arrange for their resupply. This was critical now that their location had been changed, and Sir Walter Raleigh would be unaware of it. Obviously, they could not depend on Fernando to inform him. Their ships had surely carried as many supplies as possible, but not being allowed to take on additional supplies in the West Indies as planned had reduced their store so that it was no longer adequate. Now that they could not expect any supply ships to find them until someone returned to England to give their location, they could not be sure how long their provisions would have to sustain them. They realized it was important to send a person of authority and respect to adequately express their perilous situation. Only one assistant came forward, but he alone was considered inadequate. Finally, John White was able to persuade Christopher Cooper to go, but his mind was quickly changed by his friends.

The next day, August 22, after having time to talk among themselves and give further consideration to their predicament, a group consisting of the assistants and some of the planters met with John White to convince him that he would be the most effective person to return to England to secure the necessary supplies in a timely manner. Since he had been chosen by Sir Walter Raleigh to lead the colony, they believed he would have the best access to him. White was adamantly against their plan. First, as the person instrumental in convincing many of them to come, he felt he had a responsibility to remain with the group.

He was also afraid that if he returned so soon, his political enemies would accuse him of using his experience and position to trick others to join the venture, while he really never intended to stay himself. By this time, the planters had already decided not to settle permanently on Roanoke Island, but to move 50 miles inland. White was concerned that all of his possessions would be lost or pilfered if he were absent during the move. With so many concerns, he declined to go himself.

The next day, even more of the planters, including some of the women, approached White again to try to persuade him that he was the one person best qualified to get what they needed in England. They came prepared to allay his fears. They brought with them a signed statement indicating that he did not want to leave them and only agreed to do so after they entreated him many times. They promised that they would be responsible for his goods while he was away. If his goods were spoiled in any way, they would replace them. With that assurance, White was out of excuses. He would return to England. John White's heart must have been heavily burdened as he contemplated leaving the colony on Roanoke. Nothing had gone as planned. The colony was 100 miles south of their planned destination on the mainland of the Chesapeake Bay. Supply ships would expect to find the colony there, not at Roanoke. Arriving in mid-July, they had missed the planting season and would have to depend almost entirely on the supplies they were able to bring from England. The Indians had already explained the scarcity of food due to the drought, so it was unlikely that the Croatoans would have much to share. The planters had failed at picking up additional supplies in the West Indies, which they intended to supplement the supplies they brought from England.

It appeared that White had no great concerns for the safety of the colony during his absence. He was leaving them with English leaders and their faithful friend and advisor, Manteo. He knew the friendly Croatoan Indians would do all they could to assist the colony. Apparently, he felt the greatest danger facing the colony was the lack of supplies, which he intended to remedy quickly, or he would never have left his daughter and baby granddaughter behind. White planned to get back to England as quickly as possible and return at the first opportunity.

White had only half a day to get himself ready before he left Roanoke and boarded the fly-boat on August 27. He refused to sail on the same ship as Fernando. As the two ships were weighing anchor to return to England, disaster struck the fly-boat. In the process of pulling up the anchor, a bar on the capstan broke, causing the other two bars to whip around with such force that many of the men were injured. Some would not recover.

On a second attempt, the men were so weakened by their injuries that they were unsuccessful and injured even further in the attempt. Finally, in order to keep up with the *Lion*, they were forced to cut the anchor cable. They were able to stay with the *Lion* until September 17, when they reached the Azores. With only five of the fifteen men on board the fly-boat able to stand to their duty, they were anxious to get on to England. Fernando put a few of his sailors on the fly-boat to stand in for some of the sick and injured. However, Fernando, apparently as inscrutable as ever and with no regard for the safety of the men on the flyboat, decided he would just as soon linger in the Azores for a while. Presumably, he was hoping to find a ship he could seize, or a privateering fleet he could join. So the fly-boat set out for England alone on September 18.

Trouble again plagued the fly-boat when winds proved scarce and variable. After sailing for 20 days, the fresh water supply was almost gone due to leakage. Suddenly, a storm arose out of the northeast, blowing for six days and pushing them so far off course that it took 13 days to regain their heading. Other sailors fell sick and two of them died. During this voyage, there were times that it was so cloudy that they could not use the heavens to chart their course, and they were down to just three gallons of drink which consisted of the dregs of wine and beer combined with stinking water. They expected to perish at sea.

On October 16, they made landfall near sunset and pulled into a harbor. They had no idea where they were. Their terrible condition must have been obvious, because one of the ships in the harbor sent out several men to them with water, wine, and food. It was then they learned they had reached Smerwick in west Ireland. After a couple of days to recuperate, John White and Captain Stafford rode five miles to Dingen a Cushe to get supplies for the trip to England and to get relief for the sick and injured men. Unfortunately, within a few days three of the men died, and not many days after three sick men were taken to Dingen.

John White was able to get passage on a ship leaving Dingen for England on November 1. On the same day, the fly-boat left for England manned by those sailors still alive. White arrived in England on November 5. The men in the fly-boat arrived on the November 8 and learned that the *Lion*, with its master Fernando, had arrived three weeks previously. Things had not gone well for his ship either. Not only did he arrive with no booty, but the crew had been so reduced by sickness and death that they were unable to bring the ship into harbor. They would have all died outside the harbor if a small bark had not come to their rescue. However, this earlier arrival did give Fernando the jump on John White in establishing himself in the best light with Raleigh before White had a chance to tell his story.

Whatever Fernando told Raleigh, it appears that he never sailed for Raleigh again, although he did participate in the fight against the Spanish Armada. In fact, he disappears from historical records after 1590, when he sailed with an English fleet to the Azores.

Names of the Men, Women and Children Who Arrived Safely on Roanoke Island in 1587 and Remained There

Men

John White, Governor
Roger Bailey, Ass't
Ananias Dare, Ass't
Christopher Cooper, Ass't
Thomas Stevens, Ass't
John Sampson, Ass't
Dyonis Harvie, Ass't
Roger Prat, Ass't
George Howe, Ass't
Nicholas Johnson
Thomas Warner
Anthony Cage
John Jones
John Tydway
Ambrose Viccars
Edmond English
Thomas Topan
Henry Berrye
Richard Berrye
John Spendlove
John Hemmington
Thomas Butler
Edward Powell
John Burden
James Hynde
Thomas Ellis
William Browne
Arnold Archard
John Wright
William Dutton
Maurice Allen
William Waters
Richard Kemme

Richard Arthur
John Chapman
William Clement
Robert Little
Hugh Tayler
Richard Wildye
Lewes Wotton
Michael Bishop
Henry Browne
Henry Rufoote
Richard Tomkins
Henry Dorrell
Charles Florrie
Henry Mylton
Henry Payne
Thomas Harris
William Nicholes
Thomas Phevens
John Borden
Thomas Scot
William Willes
John Brooke
Cutbert White
John Bright
Clement Tayler
William Sole
John Cotsmur
Humfrey Newton
Thomas Colman
Thomas Gramme
Marke Bennet
John Gibbes
Richard Taverner

John Stilman
Robert Wilkinson
Peter Little
John Wyles
Brian Wyles
George Martyn
Hugh Pattenson
Martyn Sutton
John Farre
John Bridger
Griffen Jones
Richard Shabedge
James Lasie
John Cheven
Thomas Hewet
William Berde
John Earnest
Henry Johnson
John Starte
Richard Darige
William Lucas
Michael Myllet
Thomas Smith

These men were assistants who did not remain in Roanoke

Simon Fernando
John Nichols
William Fullwood
James Plat
Humfrey Dimmocke

Women	Children
Eleaner Dare	John Sampson
Margery Harvie	Robert Ellis
Agnes Wood	Ambrose Viccars
Wenefred Powell	Thomas Archard
Joyce Archard	Thomas Humfrey
Jane Jones	Thomas Smart
Elizabaeth Glane	George Howe
Jane Pierce	John Prat
Audry Tappan	William Wythers
Alice Chapman	
Emma Merimoth	**Children**
------ Colman	**Born in "Virginia"**
Margaret Lawrence	
Joan Warren	Virginia Dare
Jane Mannering	---- Harvie
Rose Payne	
Elizabeth Viccars	

Indians returning from England to Roanoke Island

Manteo
Towaye

Christening of Virginia Dare

Chapter 11

Significant Information on the Fifth Voyage

It is unfortunate that John White arrived in England at a time when relations between England and Spain were volatile. Queen Elizabeth's Privy Council had just put a stay on all ships in preparation for defense against an assault by Spain. Still, Raleigh considered his colony on Roanoke as part of England's effort to thwart Spain, so he instructed Sir Richard Grenville to assemble a fleet of ships to take supplies and additional planters to Roanoke. As an immediate measure, Raleigh had a pinnace he planned to send in advance of Grenville's fleet. For some reason, the pinnace never sailed. However, Grenville was ready and waiting with a fleet of six or eight ships by the end of March 1588, but before they could sail, Grenville received an urgent message from the Privy Council warning that attack by the Spanish Armada was imminent. Grenville was ordered not to leave England with his ships.

At that point, surely White was anxious, knowing that his family and friends were expecting him to return with necessary supplies. Grenville had two small ships in his fleet that were considered unfit for military service against the Spanish Armada, a bark named *Brave* and a pinnace named *Roe*, and he had the authority to release these vessels to sail to Roanoke.

The memory of his own futile effort to resupply the colony he left with Ralph Lane may have prompted him to make these vessels available to John White to carry supplies and fifteen planters to Roanoke. The vessels were hardly suited to an Atlantic crossing, but White never got the chance to find out if they could make it.

Arriving on Roanoke Island,
5th Voyage 1590
"But we found the houses taken down and the place very strongly enclosed with a high palisado of great trees, with curtains and flankers, very fort-like; and one of the chief trees or posts at the right side of the entrance had the bark taken off, and five-foot from the ground in fair capital letters, was graven
CROATOAN,
without any cross or sign of distress..."
John White, Fifth Voyage

With all larger ships preparing for war, only the least skilled captains and crews could be spared for the voyage to Roanoke. They had hardly begun the voyage in April of 1588, when the captains began privateering and lost sight of each other. It wasn't long before the *Brave*, on which White and his planters were traveling, was intercepted by French pirates. In the skirmish, White and many others were injured and some were killed. The pirates took over the *Brave* and looted its cargo. White and those still alive on the stripped ship were barely able to make a slow return to England. The *Roe* arrived in England several weeks later. The attempt to resupply the Roanoke colony was a complete failure. With the Spanish Armada set to attack, there would be no chance of another voyage that summer. White must have felt misfortune was his constant companion. There was only one course left to John White, and it was a bitter disappointment. He would have to wait until the war was over before he could hope to secure ships suitable for making the voyage to Roanoke Island.

The English defeated the Spanish Armada in August of 1588, but it was not until March of 1590 that any further attempt was made to resupply the colonists on Roanoke. There doesn't seem to be any definite answer as to why it took so long. Perhaps Raleigh was distracted with other interests, or there may have been financial problems. It was not until Raleigh turned over more power in the venture to John White, the assistants, and other backers that anything happened.

At the end of February 1590, White was prepared to take passage with three ships funded by a London merchant and headed for the West Indies. Still hoping to resupply his colony and bring additional planters, the arrangement was that after privateering in the West Indies, the ships would stop by Roanoke long enough for John White to locate the colonists.

All was not well however, since the owner and commanders of the ships changed their minds at the last minute and would not allow White to bring any supplies or additional planters with him. This certainly did not suit White's purpose, but there was no time to go back to Sir Walter Raleigh and wait for better arrangements. So White was forced to accept their terms if he planned to have any chance to get back to America. If we can believe White's writings, he was barely tolerated on this voyage and had no authority. As anxious as he was about the planters left on Roanoke, the protracted nature of this voyage must have taken a toll on his nerves.

On March 20, 1590, the three ships, *Hopewell*, *John Evangelist*, and *Little John*, finally sailed with two small boats in tow for exploring rivers and shallow waters. On March 25, both small boats sunk due to the negligence of the boatswain. When they reached Santa Cruz, they found two large ships from London and were able to get boats from them to replace the ones they lost.

The ships sailed on to the Canaries where on April 5, they

chased and fought with a fly-boat. They killed three men and injured one. The next day they landed at Grand Canary and took on fresh water. They departed shortly and sailed on to reach Dominica the end of April.

On May 1, they were able to trade with the savages there both aboard their ships and on land. The next day the admiral ship (*Hopewell*) and the pinnace (*John Evangelist*) left Dominica, but the vice-admiral (*Little John*) stayed behind in hopes of capturing a Spanish ship bound for the Indies. The ships were to rendezvous at Hispaniola in several weeks.

The other ships sailed to the Virgin Islands where they were able to kill a large number of fowl in just a few hours. The pinnace sailed along the south side of St. John Island while the admiral ship sailed along the north side of the island. Both sailed so close to shore that the Spanish thought they were men-of-war and built the customary fires of defense along the coast.

On May 7, they landed on the northwest end of St. John Island and lay in the Yaguana River where they captured a frigate carrying hides and ginger. Pedro a Mollato, perhaps serving as a guide, deserted them for the Spanish. They departed Yaguana on May 9.

On May 13, they landed on the island of Mona. Finding about a dozen houses inhabited by the Spanish, they burned them after the Spanish fled to evade capture. The next day they sailed on, arriving on the south side of Hispaniola at the Island of Saona on May 14. Here they stayed about five days, hoping to capture Spanish ships that might choose this shorter course back to Spain.

On May 19, the vice-admiral ship (*Little John*) which they had left in Dominica, arrived at Saona. A Spanish frigate was left with that ship, and it was instructed to stay there four or five more days waiting to capture Spanish ships. The admiral ship sailed for Cape Tyburon. It was then that John White learned that the vice-admiral ship had captured two young sons of the chief in Dominica, but they managed to escape when the vice-admiral stopped at Santa Cruz Island to take in ballast.

On May 21, the admiral arrived at Cape Tyburon and found *John Evangelist* waiting for them. Here they rescued two Spaniards who were almost starved to death, because for 100 miles this area was completely desolate. The Spaniard had attracted their attention by building a fire on shore.

On May 22, their pinnace, *John Evangelist*, anchored at Cape Tyburon and the Captain explained they had been in a four hour battle with one of the King's gallies belonging to Santo Domingo. They abandoned the fight with no great harm to either side.

On May 26, the vice-admiral ship arrived in Cape Tyburon along with the frigate which had been left with it in Saona.

This was their appointed place to meet to lay in wait for Spanish ships of the Santo Domingo fleet. While there, one of the boys from the ship ran away, but returned within ten days almost starved to death. Here they discovered bones of several men they presumed had either been stragglers from the crews of other ships, or had been deposited there by men-of-war.

On June 14, they took a small Spanish frigate which had only three men aboard, who had escaped from prison in Santo Domingo. One was an expert pilot, one a mountaineer, and one a wine merchant. They were trying to get to Yaguana in Hispaniola where there were many fugitive Spaniards. The pilot told them about a ship which was taking in freight in Yaguana, so on June 17, Captain Lane was sent with his pinnace and a frigate to capture the ship.

The frigate returned on June 24 with news that Captain Lane had taken the ship, but it was not such a prize as they thought. Although there were many passengers and Negroes on board, the ship had already been raided by a French man-of-war. There were some hides, ginger, and medicinal plants still on board for their taking.

On July 2, two other ships joined the fleet at Cape Tyburon. The *Moonlight*, with Captain Edward Spicer in charge, had left England after the other ships. *Moonlight's* consort, a small pinnace named *Conclude*, accompanied *Moonlight*.

Counting the ships captured, the fleet had now grown to eight ships.

That same day the crews sighted a fleet of 14 ships of Santo Domingo and gave chase. The Spanish ships scattered so that the English had to separate to chase them, which they did until midnight. The admiral ship and the *Moonlight* came back together and caught up to the vice-admiral of the Spanish fleet. The next morning they attacked and took the ship, but they lost one man and two were hurt. They had killed four of the Spaniards and injured six. Unfortunately, with the separation during the night, the English had no idea what had become of their vice-admiral, pinnace, the two frigates, or the first prize ship they had taken.

They spent July 3 rifling and rummaging through the ship they had just captured and getting it ready to sail. They sailed on toward Cuba where they gave chase to a frigate, but lost sight of her at night.

On July 11, they reached Cape St. Anthony on the south side of Cuba, where the *Moonlight* and her pinnace were waiting for them. The men on the *Moonlight* told them that the day before they had seen a fleet of 22 ships loaded with treasure and bound for Havana.

They rested until July 22, but the weather was so still and hot that the Spaniards they had captured complained so much that they finally dropped off all but three at a place of their choice on the south side of Cuba.

On July 23, they sighted the Cape of Florida and decided to rest for two or three days and take on fresh water east of Havana. On July 26, as they were plying the waters around Havana, they spotted three small, heavily laden pinnaces headed for Havana. The pinnaces kept sailing toward them until they were within a musket shot's distance. Because the ships came so close, the English presumed they were part of their scattered fleet. So they raised their flag. Right away the ships turned around and sailed as fast as they could to shallow water near shore where the English could not follow in their ships. The English sailed on toward Florida.

They lost sight of the Coast of Florida on July 30 when they tried to pick up the swift north-running current farther at sea. On July 31, the prize ship they had taken sailed for England, the privateering portion of the journey probably being over.

From August 1 until August 9, the two remaining vessels were plagued by bad weather. They came close to Wocokon, but could not land. Finally, on August 9 the weather was good enough to get within a mile of shore, and they were able to go ashore on a small island west of Wocokon. There they collected fresh water and caught many fish.

They departed on August 12 and came to anchor at the northeast end of Croatoan where there was a break in the shore line. The next morning they sent boats out to take soundings to check the depth of the water and found it very inconsistent. They anchored at Hatorask on August 15, and saw smoke rising from Roanoke Island near the area where John White had left the colony in 1587. In the account of this voyage as published by Hakluyt, White is quoted as saying, *"At our first coming to anchor on this shore we saw a great smoke rise in the isle of Roanoke, near the place where I left our colony in the year 1587, which smoke put us in good hope that some of the colony were there expecting our return out of England...at our putting from the ship, we commanded our master gunner to make ready two minions and a falcon, well loaded, and to shoot them off with reasonable space between every shot, to the end that their reports might be heard to the place where we hoped to find some of our people."*

White immediately took the smoke as a sign that at least some of the colony was there and expecting his return. This would be consistent with his understanding with the colonists before his departure that they would probably move inland, and the reasonable expectation that when they moved, they would leave behind some men to await his return.

The next morning, John White accompanied Captain Cooke and Captain Spicer and their company with the intent to go to the place where they had seen the smoke. As they set off in the boats, they instructed the master-gunner to fire a gun at regular intervals to alert to colonists of their coming. However, before they reached shore they saw smoke rising from an area to the south and decided to go there first. As it turned out, the source of the smoke was much farther away than they imagined, and they were tired and thirsty by the time they found it. It was a disappointment. There was no sign of life or indication that anyone had been there lately. There was also no water to drink. They returned to their boats where the sailors had brought casks ashore for fresh water. They decided to delay their trip to Roanoke until the next day and set men about digging for fresh water. They returned to the ships for the night.

The next morning, August 17, they were again prepared to go to Roanoke, except they had to wait until ten o'clock before Captain Spicer returned from gathering more fresh water on shore. Captain Cooke and John White in the admiral's boat put off from the ship anchored two miles off shore and were half-way to shore before Captain Spicer's boat left. The admiral's boat had trouble passing through the breach and was almost swamped. They managed to get safely ashore, but food, powder and such were wet.

A sudden gale came out of the northeast as Captain Spicer was heading for shore, and he got caught in the breach with an unskillful master's mate who managed to let the ship be overturned by the sea, throwing the men out of the boat. They tried to hold on, but some finally let go in hopes of wading ashore.

They were beaten down and could not swim. Captain Spicer and the master's mate held onto the boat until it sunk and they were seen no more. Four men who could swim a little managed to keep to deeper water, where they were rescued when Captain Cooke and some of his men who could swim rowed out to them. 11 men were lost, including some of the chief men of the voyage.

As strange as it seems, sailors of this era made a point of not learning to swim. There are two possible reasons. The sailors knew that a wreck at sea meant certain death, and they preferred a quick death of drowning to a long painful death of dehydration. The other reason could have been that ship commanders did not encourage sailors to learn to swim so they would be less likely to abandon ship before receiving the captain's order.

After this disaster, the sailors had no interest in searching for the planters, but Captain Cooke and John White were so persuasive that they finally agreed. Once again they set off in boats for Hatorask, but by the time they got close to their destination, it was so dark that they overshot it by a quarter of a mile. They saw a large fire through the woods at the north end of the island and rowed toward it. When they got near shore, they sounded a trumpet, sang familiar English songs, and called out in a friendly manner, all to no avail. When they went ashore in the morning, they found only grass and rotten trees burning.

They went to the place where John White had left the colony. Along the shore they found only various footprints of natives in the sand. As they headed up the bank, they saw the Roman letters **"C R O"** carved on the trunk of a tree.

That was an encouraging sign to John White, since he and the planters had agreed that if they moved before his return, they would carve the name of their destination in a tree trunk or on a doorpost. There was no cross carved above the letters, which was to be the sign if they left in distress. The party continued to the houses where the colonists planned to live, but they found the houses taken down. A high palisade of large trees surrounded the place where the houses had stood. This palisade may have been necessary to keep out large animals or unfriendly Indians. The bark had been removed from one of these trees and the word **"C R O A T O A N"** carved in capital letters without any sign of distress. Inside the palisade they found bars of iron, lead, and other heavy things thrown about and overgrown with grass and weeds. They checked along the waterside near the creek to see if they could find the boats or pinnace which had been left with the planters, but they found nothing. When they returned from the creek, the sailors had discovered several chests which had been dug up and things in them scattered about. It turned out that three of the chests belonged to John White and contained his belongings. The planters had buried them in an old trench dug by Captain Amadas during Ralph Lane's venture of the Second Voyage. White's books, drawings, and maps were all spoiled and rotten. His armor was almost eaten through with rust. This was a great blow to White, since one of his main reasons for not leaving the colony to return to England was his fear that his possessions would be lost. His chests must have contained many of his drawings and maps which would have been important to history.

He blamed the damage on their enemies at Dasamonguepeuk, who he imagined had watched the departure of the planters, just waiting for the opportunity to come in and steal what they could find. The growth of weeds indicated that no one had been there for at least two seasons, and there was no evidence that the colonists had engaged in any planting of crops. On the bright side, he must have been encouraged by what he didn't find. There was no mention of finding any graves. John White consoled himself with the sure knowledge that the planters were safe in the company of their good friends, Manteo and his people, the Croatoans.

Having seen all they could at that site, the men noticed that a storm was approaching and they hurried back to the ships. The captain sent several men who could swim with a boat to pick up the casks of fresh water they had filled on shore. The storm became so intense that it was impossible for these men to get the casks loaded, and they returned to their ship without the fresh water.

The next morning brought fairer weather and the perfect winds for sailing for Croatoan (about 65 miles across Pamilco Sound) where the planters had gone. It was decided to leave the water casks on shore and collect them upon their return. As they pulled the anchor out of the water to depart, the cable broke and the anchor was lost. The winds drove them quickly towards shore, and they had to drop their third anchor, which hit bottom so quickly that they had to let the cable loose to keep from running aground. Fortunately, they slipped into a deep channel, but they were left with only the last of their four anchors. To make matters worse, the weather grew more threatening by the minute, their food supply was low, and their fresh water supply was sitting on shore where they were unable to collect it.

It was decided that the best course was to sail for St. John, or one of the other southern islands, to bring on fresh water and food. Then they would stay in the West Indies for the winter and return to Virginia in the spring. The acting captain of the *Moonlight* was afraid his ship was too leaky for such a long venture, and he sailed directly for England. The admiral ship sailed for Trinidad. For two days they sailed on course for Trinidad until August 28, when another severe storm engulfed the ship. It was impossible to keep full sails under such conditions, and the strong winds from the west blew them directly on the course for England. They surrendered to the elements and headed for the Azores. They hoped that once there they could take on fresh water and perhaps find some English men-of-war which could supply their needs. Weather conditions continued unsatisfactory, yet on September 17, they sighted two islands in the Azores, but could not anchor for the night due to a shift in the winds.

The next morning they saw a ship and gave chase, only to discover it was a Spanish ship of the Domingo fleet that had been taken already in the Indies by the their own consort ship, *Little John,* and was headed for England. They learned from the Captain of this ship that *Little John* and its pinnace had fought the rest of the Domingo fleet, forcing them into Jamaica where some ran aground, but *Little John* captured one and plundered others.

In addition, *Little John* had fought with two ships coming from Mexico headed for Havana. This was a bloody battle in which *Little John's* lieutenant was killed and the captain's right arm was shot off. Four of his men were killed and 16 injured. In the end, *Little John* took one of the Spanish ships, but it was so shot up below the waterline that it sank before its treasure, including much silver, could be removed.

The other Spanish ship was also damaged below water, but made an attempt to escape. *Little John* intended to go after it, but some of the sailors spotted galleys from Havana and Cartagena coming to the rescue of the Spanish ships, so *Little John* broke off the chase and headed for England. After relaying all of this information, the prize ship went on its way.

On September 19, White's party anchored at the island of Flores, where they found several English men-of-war as they had hoped. Some of the English informed them that *Little John* had gone on to England. One of the English ships at anchor happened to be their consort, the *Moonlight*, which set sail for England as soon as White's ship was spotted. The crew on the *Moonlight* probably feared that John White and Captain Cooke would try to convince them to join in a return voyage to Croatoan Island.

On the September 20, they realized that there was a great gathering of the Queen's fleet in the Azores, waiting for the Spanish fleet out of the West Indies. In fact, the ships were divided into two separate fleets to give them an advantage. On September 23, they were able to determine that the fleet was planning to spread out all along the coasts of Spain and Portugal to lay in wait of Spanish ships.

On September 30, they sailed for England and anchored at Plymouth on October 24, with White's notation of thanks to God. This was White's last attempt to find his Roanoke colony. He retired to Ireland comforted by the knowledge that his colony was safe with the Croatoan Indians.

Chapter 12

Incredible Chain of Events

The incredible chain of events that occurred as England attempted to plant a colony in North America shaped the earliest history of this nation, the United States of America. While England made plans to challenge Spain's influence in the New World and reap a large share of the riches for itself, two significant decisions influenced the history of North America.

First and foremost was England's claim to all of North America lying north of the thirty third and fortieth degrees of lattitude. England notified all nations that the area belonged to England, and any intrusion would be defended by its power.

Second, Queen Elizabeth chose to use a system of charters to colonize and exploit North America. Charters were granted in the name of the Queen to private citizens who financed the ventures with hope of profit. These charters were usually awarded to favorite courtiers of the Queen. So it was that Sir Walter Raleigh obtained a charter to plant a colony. By using this system of private enterprise, Queen Elizabeth planned to get England's share of the New World without draining the state coffers on risky ventures. It was a good plan, but all things were not equal.

Some ventures were better planned, managed and financed than others so that the chance of success was not the same for every enterprise. Whether or not this method was correct, it played a crucial role in the disappearance of the first colony of men, women and children who come to dwell in the new land the English named "Virginia".

In 1584, the First Voyage to "Virginia", consisted of two ships which crossed the Atlantic and sailed northward along the coast for many miles before coming to anchor in a safe harbor in an inlet that became known as Hatorask. After coming to anchor, some of the voyagers went on shore and saw a vast inland sea, and within the sea was an island. They explored the surrounding areas, were warmly welcomed and aided by the natives, and returned to England with two of those natives.

At some point the explorers came to the conclusion that the island would be a suitable place to establish a future colony. Unfortunately, their observations proved false, as it would later be the site of not one but two failed colonies.

The ships had found safe harbor on the coast of present-day North Carolina, in an area of the Atlantic known as the Graveyard of the Atlantic. The ocean floor is littered with the wrecks of ships which fell victim to the dangerous shoals jutting into the ocean, or sudden and ferocious storms that come bearing down from the northeast. These storms are known locally as Nor'easters. Other violent storms cross the Atlantic from Africa and roll over the shores as hurricanes.

This error in the selection of the colony site was another link in the incredible chain of events.

The Second Voyage was in 1585. At first, the natives willingly supplied the Englishmen with food and taught them how to set fish traps. In return, the Englishmen displayed an attitude of superiority, and their treatment of the natives was often deplorable. The natives became disenchanted with this group of Englishmen. They realized that they could not fight the Englishmen in open warfare, so they devised another plan, starvation.

The plan was succeeding, and the Englishmen were in a desperate situation when Providence intervened. Sir Frances Drake was sailing along the Atlantic coast with a large fleet and decided to stop at Roanoke Island to check on the Englishmen. Plans were made in which Drake would provide the Englishmen with supplies and a large ship so that they could continue the settlement. Many leaders of the group were on Drake's ship when a sudden storm arose and Drake moved his ships farther out in the ocean into deeper water. To the men still on shore, it appeared they were being left behind, and they made great haste to board another ship to join the others at sea. The storm destroyed several small boats, as well as the ship Drake intended to leave for Lane's colony. After that, it was decided that tarrying in the midst of the storm was a danger to the ships, so the whole fleet sailed away with the colonists, creating another link in the incredible chain of events.

Adding to the incredible chain of events, Raleigh was concerned enough about the colony to send a single supply ship ahead of Grenville's supply fleet. That ship arrived at Roanoke immediately after Lane and his men sailed away with Sir Frances Drake. Finding no one on Roanoke Island when the supply ship arrived, the captain sailed back to England.

About two weeks after the supply ship went back to England, Grenville arrived with his own supply ships. He made a thorough search of the area, but found no one. He left fifteen men behind to keep possession of the country and sailed away. If Lane's colonists had only waited a few days longer, history would have been different.

Another attempt at colonization was in 1587 when a group of men, women, and children arrived at Roanoke Island rather than their intended destination in the Chesapeake Bay area. When their pilot refused to take them any farther, they convinced the Governor of the colony, John White, to return to England to secure the necessary supplies and report their new location.

Upon arriving in England he discovered that Queen Elizabeth had forbidden any ships to leave the country due to rising tensions with Spain and the possibility of war. Governor John White could not return to his colony at Roanoke until 1590, another link in the chain.

The Spanish already had information about the English settlement, but their information indicated that it was in the Chesapeake Bay area. A Spanish ship sailed from Florida to that area in the spring of 1588, looking for the colony. Finding nothing, the ship was returning to Florida when it took refuge from a storm behind the Outer Banks. When the storm passed, the captain discovered a slipway and other signs that a sizeable colony had been on Roanoke Island but had deserted the location. John White was not aware of this information when he later sailed back to Roanoke Island in hopes of finding his colony.

When he finally returned to Roanoke Island, the ships in that fleet anchored off the northeast end of Croatoan Island on the evening of August 12, before reaching Roanoke several days later. If John White had only known then that he would find information on Roanoke Island directing him to Croatoan Island, surely he would have insisted on a search of Croatoan Island while they were anchored there.

At last, White came ashore on Roanoke Island where he found information indicating the colonists had gone to Croatoan Island. White returned to the ships and planned to sail the next day to that location. However, in the evening a sudden storm arose, continuing throughout the night and damaging the ships. The Captain refused to allow the ships to tarry any longer, and Governor White was unable to act upon the message left by the colonists to search for them on Croatoan Island.

White never again was able to fund another search for the colonists. The storm which prevented Governor White's search is yet another link in the chain of incredible events.

After five voyages to Virginia without locating the desired riches, funds from private sources became unavailable. Under the terms of the charter, the English government had no obligation to offer aid. Therefore no extensive efforts were made to locate the colony. The charter system England used for exploration added another link to the chain of events that shaped the early history of America.

It is incredible that during the years of attempts at settlement so many events occurred and at such times that doomed the success of John White's colony. The use of charters for settlement, two severe storms, the misguided authority of sea captains, and circumstances related to war between England and Spain all played important roles in the destiny of the colony. When one adds the lack of communication, meager knowledge of weather and climate patterns in the area, and scanty information about the land and the coastline, surely the odds against success were high. Fate showed its cruel face to the colonists in an incredible chain of events.

Chapter 13

The Case for Survival of the Colonists

History records only that the colonists who arrive on Roanoke Island in 1587, disappeared from the island and were never seen again. The popular assumption is that they were killed by Indians. But what if that assumption is wrong? There is no direct evidence that the colonists were killed. There were no bodies found, no bones and no signs of battle. Without direct evidence, it should not be assumed that they perished. The direct evidence indicates that their departure was planned in advance and was for a very logical reason. A correct conclusion regarding the fate of the Lost Colony requires a close look at the facts of history, a detailed examination of the original documents, a respect for truths passed through the traditions of oral history, an understanding of human nature, and a reasonable amount of common sense.

Looking at the historical documents of the voyage of 1587, it is clear that the intended destination was the Chesapeake Bay, where twenty years later the successful Jamestown Colony was planted. When the colonists landed on Roanoke Island, they had no plan to remain there permanently. It was intended as a stopover to allow them to check on the 15 men who had been left there on the previous voyage.

The original plan for the voyage of 1587 was for the ships to stop in Hispanola to resupply before continuing to the Chesapeake Bay. This was common practice for voyages, but for unexplained reasons, no supplies were acquired on the stops in the West Indes.

When the colonists finally reached the coast of North Carolina, their supplies were lower than planned. As John White and a party of men were going ashore, Captain Fernando ordered his sailors not to bring them back to the ship, as he feared bad weather and wanted to return immediately to England rather than take them to Chesapeake Bay. Only John White and a few of his assistants were allowed back aboard. In this situation, there was little alternative for the colonists. They prevailed upon John White to return to England with Captain Fernando and return with supplies.

According to his own records, White indicated it was anticipated that the colonists would relocate before he returned from England with supplies. White and the colonists agreed upon a plan should they decide to leave the area before his expected return in three months. They were to carve the name of their destination on a tree trunk so he would know where to find them. Indeed, when he finally did return three years later, White himself said he was greatly relieved to find the word **CROATOAN** carved on a post of their fort.

He had also instructed them to carve a Maltese cross above the word if they had left under duress. He did not find a cross.

It is reasonable to assume that people brave enough to leave behind family, friends and the life they knew to come to a vast and largely unknown land would be resourceful and tenacious in making a success in the New World. Not only John White, but one or two other voyagers, had previously sailed to Roanoke Island. They would have had ample time on the voyage from England to discuss with the colonists all they had learned of the Indian methods of survival and the Indian culture. It should not be assumed that they knew nothing of surviving in America, and they certainly would have been aware that the Indians were their best resource.

The records of previous voyages related that the Indians were known to travel from place to place when necessary to follow the food supply. They traveled in small village-size groups that would not disturb other indians or deplete resources. It is possible that the colonists saw the wisdom of such an arrangement and split into smaller groups when they reached Croatoan, before moving to the mainland to explore suitable places for a colony. Some of these small groups may have joined with their Indian friends and followed them inland. Perhaps they planned to regroup when the next season again brought the Indians to Croatoan.

If a group of the colonists joined with Indians and headed for the Chesapeake Bay area, that would be one explanation for the statement of other Englishman regarding sightings of non-Indians in that area years later. It would also shed some light on the statement of Powhatan that he had slaughtered the Englishmen of Roanoke. If his statement were true, it could have been only a small group of the colonists entering his territory. On the other hand, it may have been only an outlandish brag to intimidate the English who came in later years, as he saw that more and more of them would be coming to his territory.

The Spanish were well entrenched in Central America and even had a garrison in the area now known as Florida. Historical Spanish records indicate the Spanish in Florida were aware of the colony in Virginia, and in fact sent a search party to find them. Fortunately, they believed the colonists to be in the Chesapeake Bay area, but the colonists may have spotted the Spanish ships sailing past as they scanned the horizon for a returning English ship. Aware of the Spanish reputation for brutality to anyone standing in their way, the colonists may have decided it was time to move to the mainland where they were not as exposed.

The coast of North Carolina has long been known as the "Graveyard of the Atlantic", because of the unpredictable hurricanes and northeastern storms that rage in the coastal waters.

We know from historical records that many ships went down in this area when returning to Europe loaded with treasure from the New World. John White wrote that it was one of these storms that prevented him from making a thorough search for the colonists on his return voyage. Other adventurers who promised to search were also prevented by storms. It may be that such fierce weather conditions convinced the colonists that coastal islands such as Roanoke and Croatoan were not the best place for a colony to survive when they could easily move to the mainland as the Indians made their migration.

We know from scientific studies that the period when the colonists arrived at Roanoke was a time when a serious drought was affecting the area. In an article entitled "If It's Not One Thing, It's Another (Weather and Climate for the Roanoke Colony)", Dennis B. Blanton makes this statement. *"...there are occasional suggestions of drought-induced hardship. The clearest comes when John White describes the initial reunion of the English and Indians during July 1587. White relates that the natives immediately expressed concern about their lack of corn: 'Some of them (the Indians) came to us embracing and entertaining us friendly, desiring us not to gather or spoil any of their corn, because they had but little.'"*

Mr. Blanton also points out that the sandy soils of these thin coastal strands not only drain quickly, but have limited reservoirs of potable groundwater accessible to shallow wells. *"Drinkable surface water was likewise scarce, probably even in the best of times, as John White's 1590 account of an island exploration following the drought period attests: '(N)or had we found any fresh water in all this way to drink....The sailors in our absence had brought their cask ashore for fresh water, so we deferred our going to Roanoke until the next morning, and caused some of them to dig in the sandy hills for fresh water – which we found very sufficient.' Suffice it to say that a drought very likely all but erases surface water sources and reduced the volume and quality of shallow wells in the sandy island soils."*

The article cites a study by David Stahle of the University of Arkansas of an eight-hundred-year-long-tree-ring record for that area. The study found that there was a severe drought in 1587–1589. Perhaps this scarcity of food and water made it necessary for the colonists to move inland when John White did not return for three years.

Much is made of the probability that hostile Indians killed the colonists, but records indicate that only a small number of Indians were hostile. The majority were welcoming, helpful and friendly. It seems reasonable that the Indians at Croatoan would have known how to avoid hostiles, and would have been glad to take their English friends to safety, especially since the advanced weaponry that the English possessed would have made it to their advantage.

It is difficult to understand the mindset of the colonists when we are so accustomed to instant communication, but their world turned at a much different pace. They were not accustomed to regular mail service, and it would not be unusual to go for months or even years without communication with family or friends in distant places. Nor was it unusual for someone to embark upon a journey never to be heard from again. Life was precarious. After enduring the separation from all they knew and those they loved to cross an enormous sea in small ships powered only by sails and facing dangers of storms and pirates, the colonists were not likely to simply perish waiting to be rescued. They would not give up easily on making a life in this new land. They were survivors!

During the three years with no sight of John White and no word of what was happening in Europe, the colonists surely concluded that help was not coming, and they would have to make the best of things on their own in the new land. The Indians were prone to move about, and the colonists may have adopted their lifestyle while on Croatoan and followed the Indians when they left the area.

Chapter 14

The Indians Encountered by the Colonists

David Beers Quinn in his book, **The Lost Colonists – Their Fortune and Probable Fate**, gives an in-depth look at the Indian culture at the time the English colonists first arrived in the area they called Virginia. A thorough reading of his information quickly dispels the common notion of undisciplined, blood-thirsty savages which so often inhabits fictional writing and colors our imagination.

Author Quinn described North America not as a wilderness, but as a land inhabited for thousands of years by native people who cleared hunting grounds in the forest, prepared plots of land for growing crops, and constructed villages which were connected by a system of trails. We know from the reports of the voyages and John White's drawings that their villages were laid out in an orderly fashion and that some of them could be moved quickly when necessary. The natives maintained gardens for growing food crops such as corn and squash, and they used fish weirs and dugout canoes (made from burned out tree trunks) in order to provide fish and crustaceans to supplement their diet. Skillful in the use of bows and arrows, they killed wild animals and birds for food. The Indians also collected roots, wild fruit and nuts.

The historical reports reveal that the natives had an organized culture and religion. They had developed relationships among their various local groups and were in contact with groups at great distances. Each group had a structured hierarchy, with a ruling family at the top. Although their weapons were inferior to those of the English, the native men were formidable fighters with the weapons they possessed and at times engaged in battle to protect or expand their territory.

Quinn's description of the division of work among the Indians is supported by historical reports and drawings. The men were responsible for site clearing, house building, hunting and fishing. The women tended gardens, cooked, prepared food to store for winter, and made pottery, mats, baskets, as well as all of the clothing.

Unlike the previous colony, the Lost Colony was not military in nature, but was a mixed group of families and skilled workmen determined to build a new life in "Virginia". We know that the natives were not xenophobic, and this small number of people did not present a threat to the indigenous people. Quinn was convinced that their chances of being well treated by the natives were good.

He concluded that, "The Lost Colonists disappeared, therefore, into a land already inhabited and developed, where they might assimilate or remain separate. Their fate and fortune lay in the hands of the native people."

Virginia Indian Running
(Engraving by Theodor de Bry from a
drawing by John White)

Chapter 15

What Became of the Lost Colony?

If one is to make correct assumptions about what became of the English of the Lost Colony, it is essential to identify with the colonists in their era and in their surroundings. Their lives were so different from ours in almost every way that it is difficult to see the world from their point of view. Once they departed England, information about the affairs of the world, other than their immediate location, was not available to them and would have had no effect on their decisions.

With the 24/7 news cycle of today, that isolation from the world can be a little frightening, but it wasn't to the colonists. It was normal. They were not accustomed to daily newspapers, regular mail service, or daily contact with anyone outside their immediate vicinity. Very few had any part in the political affairs of the day, or a broad knowledge of the world as far as it had been discovered. Their lives and social position were regulated by numerous laws and, they had little time for contemplation of matters outside their small sphere of family and friends. Maintaining a roof over their heads and putting food on the tables and clothes on their backs were their main concerns. Their children were expected to assume responsibilities at a young age, and self-reliance was essential for all.

They made their decisions based on experience and common sense. Too often the colonists are viewed from a modern perspective and cast in the role of victims rather than seen as resourceful, determined people intent on creating a life of freedom and limitless possibility in a beautiful and bountiful new land.

In an age when maps of the New World were imprecise and weather patterns were not well understood, any voyage was full of uncertainty. Yet the colonists were willing to endure a long voyage in small, cramped ships with almost no privacy in order to establish a colony in a relatively unexplored land three thousand miles from their home. Along the way, it was likely they would encounter privateers who would steal all they had, or their enemies, the Spanish, who might imprison them or even kill them. Unquestionably, the colonists were not people who would easily succumb to difficult circumstances. They possessed the mettle and resolve to meet with vigor any challenge they faced.

The original roster of colonists totaled one hundred fifty. However, in the time it took to make all of the necessary arrangements for the ships to depart, the list of those actually sailing had dwindled to one hundred eighteen. Lack of finances no doubt eliminated some, while the delay gave others time to reconsider and to decide that the risks were too high.

Those who finally set sail had chosen to sever ties with all that was familiar in order to embrace the adventure of opening a new country where they could create for themselves the kind of lives which were out of reach for them in England. They were willing to face the rigors and uncertainty of a long sea voyage for the promise of creating a new society in which they would be the masters of their fates. Most of the colonists probably expected never to return to England, and they knew they would have to depend on their own resources and each other in order to survive in the new country. Their future was ahead of them in Virginia, whatever that future turned out to be.

When the ships made a scheduled stop at Roanoke Island to check on the fifteen men left behind the previous year to "hold the fort", their pilot, Simon Fernando, forced everyone ashore and would not allow them back aboard. This was an inexplicable act, unless someone with authority had already decided that trade and privateering were the priorities of this voyage rather than colonization. This idea is supported by the fact that although these colonists were expecting to settle in the Chesapeake Bay area, no advance party had been sent to Chesapeake Bay to determine a good location for a colony. That would seem to be a vital preparation for establishing a permanent colony.

It is said that the best judge of a person's character is his actions rather than his words. We get a good sense of the type of people the colonists were by observing their actions upon arrival at Roanoke Island, when their pilot forced them to disembark at a location already determined by the previous colonists to be unsuitable for establishing a permanent colony. John White did not report anyone losing his temper or being unduly distressed, despite the major and unexpected change in their original destination of the Chesapeake Bay. Common sense prevailed. White and a party of men simply carried out their instructions to check on the status of the fifteen men left behind by Grenville on the previous voyage. The others made the best of their situation, setting about repairing the abandoned houses left from the previous settlement on the northeastern end of the island near the fort Ralph Lane had constructed during his expedition the previous year. They would also have started building new ones to provide housing for all of their company.

The houses which Lane's men built on Roanoke Island were probably one-and-a half or two story houses, judging by the reference to "neather rooms of them", meaning beneath or below. They may have had brick foundations and chimneys. Darby Glande, who had been a member of Ralph Lane's 1585 colony, joined the 1587 voyage as well, but left that voyage in Puerto Rico. He later testified before the Spanish about the activities of the 1585 voyage. According to him, "as soon as they had disembarked (at Roanoke) they began to make brick and fabric for a fort and houses".

As late as 1860, pieces of brick were reportedly found at the site. More recently, archaeologists have found brickbats that possibly date to the Elizabethan period. However, no evidence has been found of extensive brick work. That plus John White's statement that he found the houses of the colonists "taken down" when he returned in 1590, indicates the main building material was flat boards. We know those on the voyage of 1585 had a forge which was used for making nails, and it is most certainly something which would have been useful to future colonists. It is just the type of equipment that Ralph Lane's party would have left behind in their hasty departure in 1586. It is safe to assume that the houses had thatched roofs, because of Ralph Lane's report that under cover of darkness, the Indians "would have beat my house, and put fire in the reeds that the same was covered with". We know that the 1585 voyage included carpenters, thatchers, and brickmakers who were expected to construct dwellings for Lane's men.

With the unexpected change of locations for founding their "Cittie of Raleigh", the immediate needs of the colonists became their priority, and it is likely that they felt fortunate to have some houses already available with winter not far away.

Had the colonists been put ashore in the Chesapeake Bay area, they would have had no accommodations waiting for them. It would have been necessary for the ships to remain in the bay to provide shelter for as long as it took to construct new houses for the colonists, assuming Simon Fernando would have been willing to do so. What must have seemed a major deviation from their plans actually may have been a blessing. Twenty years later when the Jamestown Colony settled on the Chesapeake Bay, they had much time to consider the difficulties of Sir Walter Raleigh's efforts at colonization before they set out, as well as what improvements they might make for a successful effort. Yet that colony very nearly perished from exposure, disease, and starvation even though they were resupplied. If the Roanoke Colonists had been delivered to the Chesapeake Bay as planned, but without resupply and without the help of friendly Indians already known to them, it is likely they would have perished.

John White and the leaders of the colony followed Sir Walter Raleigh's instructions, christening Manteo as the first native American to become a Christian and conferring upon him the title of "Lord of Roanoke and Dasamonguepeuk", the territory which belonged to the hostile and now deceased Wingina. A few days later, Eleanor Dare, the wife of Ananias Dare and daughter of John White, gave birth to a baby girl. Since this baby was "the first Christian" born in Virginia, she was christened Virginia Dare. She was the first American citizen born of English descent.

Whatever their disappointments, the colonists were able to adjust to adversity and keep moving forward. Based upon sentiments later expressed by John White, it may well have been that they believed their fates were in the hands of the Almighty God and simply trusted in his perfect will for them. They did not complain or lose heart. Why should they? They were surely awe struck, stepping ashore in an immense and glorious virgin land. How their spirits must have soared with the sense that they possessed more freedom than any other Englishman. They were home.

When it was clear that someone must return to England for needed supplies, it would have been perfectly understandable if many disappointed and disgruntled colonists rushed forward to volunteer. After all, hardly anything had gone as planned, and the colonists had arrived too late in the year to plant the crops they were counting on to supplement their supplies. As amazing as it might be to the modern mind, only one person volunteered, and he soon changed his mind. It seemed no one wanted to return to England. It was only after much pleading that the colonists finally convinced John White that he was the one most suited to return to England to represent them.

John White gives a glimpse into his character by his reaction to being asked to abandon his other duties as governor and sail back to England for supplies.

He did not protest another long and dangerous voyage with the tedious pilot, Fernando, or complain about the months he would be separated from his daughter and new grandchild. He did not even express concern that the colony might not get the best start without his leadership.

Amid circumstances that most people would consider disastrous, White's main concern was for the good of the colony. He feared that his return to England so soon would bring disgrace on him for abandoning the people he had convinced to go to Virginia, and that seeming disinterest would have negative consequences in securing the necessary continuing support for the colony. When the colonists finally succeeded in persuading him that he was the only one capable of quickly securing and delivering the supplies needed, White set aside his own comfort, any personal ambition, and his desires for seeing his colony off to a good start in order to do what he felt was necessary for the good of all. He seemed to console himself with making sure his writings, drawings and other personal effects, which probably represented a large part of his assets, would be preserved in his absence. Had he known what a great resource his writings and drawings would become to understanding the history of that period, perhaps preparations for preserving them would have been more of a concern.

White demonstrated the resolve and strength of character which were apparently common among the colonists from the beginning. It should be noted that any fear for the safety of the colonists during his absence was not mentioned as one of his concerns. It appears that nothing in his past or present experiences made him afraid that harm would come to them.

John White did not record any sign of hostility from the Indians when his colonists arrived on Roanoke Island. As a matter of fact, they didn't encounter any Indians at first. In the days before John White's departure, a colonist, George Howe, was killed when he foolishly left camp and went fishing alone. The small group of hostile Indians who killed him was previously led by the deceased Wingina. Most likely, Wanchese, the Indian who accompanied Manteo to England in 1584, had taken Wingina's place as their leader.

Unlike Manteo, Wanchese's experiences in England had turned him against the English and made him view them as a threat to his people. The killing of Howe and three of the English left by Grenville no doubt were in retaliation for what Wanchese perceived as wrongs against his people. The Croatan Indians informed the colonists that those hostile Indians had left Roanoke Island the previous year to live on the mainland. While John White was quickly organizing a party of men for a pre-dawn retaliation against those hostile Indians, Manteo's people had gone to the deserted camp site on the mainland and were there searching for food.

In the darkness before dawn, John White and his men did not recognize their friends, the Croatoan Indians, and unfortunately some were injured before the mistake became clear. Even so, Manteo maintained his allegiance to the English and declared it was due to the folly of the Croatoan Indians themselves that any of them were injured. The Indians showed no anger or resentment toward the English because of this mistake and told White that the hostile Indians had fled the area immediately after killing George Howe. The colonists' understanding of that event apparently satisfied them that the killing of Howe was out of the ordinary and involved only a small number of hostile Indians.

In spite of strained relations that developed between a small group of Indians and the English over the year that the previous colonists lived on Roanoke Island (1585-1586), John White had no hesitation in bringing his own daughter to Virginia and leaving her and her infant on Roanoke Island when he returned to England. John White's drawings from the previous voyage show that he was a keen observer and friend of the Indians, and he surely would have known if any sizeable group of Indians had dangerously hostile feelings toward the English.

During the time that Ralph Lane spent in the Roanoke Island area, he visited with the native King Menatonon, whose territory included the Pamlico Sound area, and received a great deal of useful information from him.

Menatonon was the only native King to receive such a visit, and a friendship between the two leaders was quickly established.

It is not unreasonable to assume that Manteo acted as Lane's guide as he had done on other occasions. No doubt Manteo excitedly informed Menatonon of all the wonders he had seen in England, as well as the impressive military skills of the English which he witnessed during the 1585 voyage from England to America. Menatonon was impressed enough that at a later time he sent word to King Okisko, who was King of several villages along the northern shore of Albermarle Sound, to honor Queen Elizabeth and her subjects, and Okisco accepted that. With Menatonon, Okisko, and the Croatoans bearing friendly feelings for the colonists and the small group of hostile Indians having already fled the area, John White must have felt he was leaving his colony in a very safe place.

There is no account of what went on during the time John White's colony remained on Roanoke Island, but it is likely that Manteo, in his new position as Lord of Dasamonguepeuk and Roanoke, immediately established his authority and aligned the Indians of the area under his leadership. Manteo was certainly a high ranking person in his own culture, or the leaders of the First Voyage would never have taken him back to England for education.

Manteo and his people on Croatoan Island were under the authority of King Menatonon, but there is no record of those on the First Voyage ever meeting King Menatonon.

There is reason to believe that Manteo's mother was related to Menatonon and was head of the Indians on Croatoan Island. Therefore, we may assume that Manteo was of such a superior ranking that he was able to make the decision to go to England when the First Voyage returned. As an astute leader, Manteo was anxious to learn as much as he could about the English, realizing that their advanced culture could benefit his people. History does not record all that Manteo did and saw while in England, but as such a fascinating representative of the people of the New World, there is no doubt he was grandly entertained with such traditional English pastimes as horseback riding, hunting, feasting, music and dancing.

For one who was not familiar with rudimentary science and technology, Manteo must have been astounded by such things as a compass, wheeled vehicles, large stone buildings and bridges. We know that he lived in Sir Walter Raleigh's house on the Thames River, possibly at other of Raleigh's homes, where under the tutelage of Thomas Harriot, who was on the First Voyage, he learned to speak English, to adopt English manners, and to dress in the English fashion. During his stay in England he was presented at court and received much attention from the nobility. He surely learned many useful skills which aren't documented, but which set him apart as highly superior to any other Indian leader. In addition, it was apparent that the English were his friends, and it would have been clear that whether out of fear or out of respect, there was great advantage to following the Indian most loved and honored by the English.

Even when White did not return to Roanoke Island on schedule, the colonists probably felt no undue concern. There was no definite timetable for making the trip, and they had experienced a very long voyage themselves. Generally, two months would have been a good crossing, but sailing the Atlantic was full of uncertainties, and winter was not the optimum time for a voyage. Six months would not have been unusual for the round trip. Also, they would have considered the possibilities that White's ship may have sunk in a storm. John White's map of the coast of Virginia even depicted several sunken ships. They would have concerns that White's ship may have been captured by the Spanish. They were aware of the tensions between England and Spain before they left England. There was always the danger of ships being taken by privateers. In spite of the known dangers, no doubt it was just another disappointment when White did not return as planned, but there would have been no panic. From the point of view of the colonists, it was just as likely he had been delayed with bureaucracy in dealing with the financial backers or the crown. Even if the worst occurred and White had never reached England, the colonists would assume one of the other ships probably made it and alerted Sir Walter

Raleigh to their change of location and their need of supplies. The fact is that the Roanoke colonists were never waiting to be "rescued" as so many historians and researchers wrongly assume when they cast the colonists as victims. They simply were waiting to be resupplied.

When John White returned to England, his efforts were directed toward gathering supplies for the colony as quickly as possible and even enlisting additional "planters" to add to the colony. The fact that he planned to take additional people to Roanoke makes it certain that it was never his intention to rescue those left on Roanoke Island and return them to England.

After several unsuccessful attempts at making contact with the colonists he left behind, John White, who best knew them and their circumstances, had this to say to his friend Hakluyt on February 4, 1593, when he despaired of ever being able to mount another voyage to bring them aid. *"Thus committing the relief of my discomfortable company, the planters in "Virginia", to the merciful help of the Almighty, whom I most humbly beseech to help and comfort them, according to His most holy will, and their good desire, I take my leave."* (Hakluyt) Still foremost in John White's mind was "relief", not rescue.

After the evidence he found on Roanoke Island upon his returned in 1590, John White did not think the colonists had perished. In his account of this voyage as published by Hakluyt, White stated that,*"on the 15th of August, toward evening we came to anchor at Hattorask in 36 1/3, in five fathoms of water, three leagues from shore. At our first coming to anchor on this shore we saw a great smoke rise in the isle of Roanoke, near the place where I left our colony in the year 1587, which smoke put us in good hope that some of the colony were there expecting our return out of England."*

This clearly indicates that there must have been a plan made before White left the colony that a portion of the colony would move to another location, but *"some of the colony were there expecting our return out of England"*.

It makes perfect sense that when they departed, the colonists planned to leave at least a small party behind, probably on Croatoan Island, to wait for White's return and guide him to their new location. If John White had ever searched on Croatoan Island, it seems certain that information about the colonists' ultimate destination would have been found.

There have been numerous accounts throughout even modern history of individuals and small groups disappearing and being given up for dead only to reappear even decades later. A disappearance is not synonymous with death. When we accept that mindset, we are more likely to be successful in determining the most reasonable scenario of what became of the lost colonists.

POINT: The Roanoke colonists were not frightened victims. Regardless of an unexpected change of plans, they were self-reliant people who intended to make Virginia their home. They carried out their instructions and duties in an orderly manner and formulated plans to ensure their survival, even including a move to a more favorable location.

The Colonists Had Some Advantages

Things had not gone as planned for the colonists left on Roanoke Island in 1587. Even so, there were a few things in their favor. Perhaps their most important asset was Manteo, the Indian who had returned to his homeland on the voyage with them. Not only had he been christened into the Christian faith, but he had been given by Sir Walter Raleigh's orders the title of "Lord of Roanoke and Dasamonguepeuk" as a reward for his faithfulness to the English. Both of these events would have bound Manteo even more strongly to the colonists. During his visits to England and his association with Englishmen, Manteo had become a great admirer of the English. By the time he was left on Roanoke Island with the English colonists, he must have been feeling quite like one of them and would have felt a great responsibility for their survival.

A few of the men in the group, including Captain Stafford, had participated in the 1585 exploration and attempt at colonization at Roanoke. During that year, these men would certainly have acquired valuable survival skills, as well as knowledge of the territory and the Indians. It seems reasonable to assume they would also have learned at least a small vocabulary of Indian words for basic communication. No doubt much time during the tedious days of the long voyage of 1587 had been spent teaching a basic vocabulary of Indian words to the colonists so they could communicate with the two natives on board.

Manteo, John White, the men from the previous colony, and Towayne, another Indian who had been taken to England and was now returning home, would have been the instructors.

In addition to the houses the previous colonists built, they must have dug at least one well, and they built a slipway for boats. John White's colonists would not have had these advantages if they had gone to the Chesapeake Bay.

John White's watercolors show that he viewed the Indians as noble, friendly people, and he had a great deal of respect for them. He could not have helped but impart this attitude to the other colonists during their long voyage when he was telling them all about the land and the people in their new home. By the time they arrived at Roanoke Island, the colonists related to the Indians as respected friends and not as arrogant commanders like Grenville and Lane did on the Second Voyage. Surely, that attitude would have gone far in reassuring the Indians of the peaceful nature of their presence and their desire to renew the bond of friendship between them.

Having women and children in the group created a different dynamic from previous voyages. The interaction between the Indian and English women involved in daily chores would have drawn them together and created a strong bond of support, as those of each culture learned from the other. No doubt the English and Indian children spent their free time playing together.

English boys would have been fascinated by miniature bows and arrows of the Indian boys, while the girls may have shared their dolls. The English children probably enlisted the Indian children in their games of blind man's bluff, marbles and hopscotch. Perhaps the Indian boys taught the English boys to swim. It would have been clear that this was not a military expedition. The colonists were there to live among the Indians as friends and neighbors.

POINT: The colonists were most fortunate to have the basic elements of a community in place when they arrived. They had shelter, food and water. In addition, the natives they encountered were not strangers, but the family and friends of Manteo, the high ranking native who was a strong friend of the English. From John White's drawings and descriptions, the English were predisposed to respecting and befriending the Indians on Roanoke Island. The fact that they arrived with families would have created an atmosphere encouraging friendships.

What Went Wrong?

Considering that establishing a permanent colony in Virginia was crucial to England's plans for becoming a presence in the New World, every effort should have been made to resupply the colonists left on Roanoke Island in 1587. However, the colony seems to have been a casualty of conflicting crises.

Queen Elizabeth I had managed to give great offense to Spain, first by supporting the Netherlands in its resistance to Spanish rule, and secondly by rejecting a proposed matrimonial alliance between Elizabeth and Spain's monarch, Philip. Spain was already a formidable naval power with allies who would support her in a war against England. When the Spanish Armada threatened England with 140 ships and 30,000 men just as John White was asking for ships to resupply the colony, it is not hard to understand the pressure Queen Elizabeth felt to send every available ship against the Spanish who were only too eager to teach her a lesson. She must have felt an obligation to the colonists, but the New World was over 3,000 miles across the Atlantic Ocean, and England was only beginning to explore and settle it. On the other hand, the Spanish threat to England was immediate and critical. If the colony failed, there would be other opportunities, but if England failed against the Spanish Armada, it would mean disaster. She refused to let any ships leave England that might be useful in sea battle. It must have been a calculated sacrifice for Queen Elizabeth, weighing the lives of just over 100 brave colonists against the future of her kingdom.

John White did everything in his power to resupply his colony. Soon after he returned to England, Sir Walter Raleigh was anxious to send immediate help and to provide a pinnace to carry supplies and additional "planters" to the colony on Roanoke Island.

The reason is not clear, but the pinnace never sailed. With the Spanish ships readying for war, it may have been too dangerous for a single ship to attempt the voyage.

Although it took longer, Sir Richard Grenville had been preparing a fleet of ships to carry supplies to the colony. He was almost ready to sail when Queen Elizabeth sent word that his ships were needed to fight the Spanish Armada and must remain in port. There were two small ships in Grenville's supply fleet that were too small and lacked the maneuverability to be useful in sea battle. So Grenville gave John White a bark, the *Brave*, and a pinnace, the *Roe* to resupply the colony. Unfortunately, any skilled commanders or pilots were needed for service on the ships preparing for war, and John White set sail for his colony with two small ships commanded by men of questionable skill and intent on privateering rather than reaching the colony on Roanoke Island. After spending a week and a half engaging in privateering activities, the *Brave* and the *Roe* were separated. French ships overtook the *Brave*, stripped it of anything useful, and damaged it badly in the process. The *Brave* limped back to England, followed later by the *Roe*. The ships never began the Atlantic crossing. There would be no voyage to Roanoke Island in 1588, or for another year and a half.

After England's decisive victory over the Spanish Armada in August 1588, the best season for sailing to Roanoke Island, the spring, was past. Considering John White's determination to resupply his colony, that may not have been the only reason a ship was not sent at once. Many believe that Raleigh's penchant for dabbling in too many things at once distracted him. Perhaps one of his many other interests became more exciting to him as a diversion after the strain of battle defeating the Spanish Armada. Raleigh loved the excitement of new ventures, but often lacked the perseverance to see them through. Or it may have been that his complicated personal life threatened his standing with the Queen and demanded all of his attention. In any case, Raleigh had definitely lost interest. So much so that in the spring of 1589, he transferred his trading rights in Virginia to a group of men including John White, his assistants in the colony, and Richard Hakluyt. With White now having an even greater share in the colony, and presumably more authority to command action, why wasn't a supply ship sent out immediately? There is no definitive answer. John White did not return to his colony for more than two and a half years after he left it.

Even when he made the return voyage to the "Cittie of Raleigh" in March of 1590, it was not under the best circumstances. There were three ships in the fleet, *Hopewell*, *Little John* and *John Evangelist* (*Moonlight* would join them later in the Caribbean), but John White seems to have been no more than a passenger with no authority. Once again, the first priority of the fleet was privateering instead of resupply of the Roanoke Colony. The voyage lasted over four months before the fleet's two remaining vessels, *Hopewell* and *Moonlight,* finally approached Roanoke Island. It was evening and the captains were afraid of dangerous shoals, so the ships lay off shore all night. The next day was wasted looking for the source of smoke they saw on a sand bank.

When they finally set out for Roanoke Island on the third day, disaster struck! While two boats navigated through the inlet, a sudden storm overturned one, drowning seven men, including Captain Spicer of the *Moonlight.* Not surprisingly, the sailors did not want to continue across the sound to Roanoke Island, but under stern orders from their remaining captain, they did. Reaching Roanoke Island at dark, they spent the night in their boats and went ashore in the morning. They found no sign of life on the island. What they found were the letters "CRO" carved on a tree and "CROATOAN" carved on a doorpost of the fort. These were certain signs to John White that his colonists had moved to Croatoan Island south of Roanoke Island. Finding no cross, the prearranged sign of distress, with the carvings, White was assured all was well. He wrote, *"I greatly joyed that I had safely found a certain token of their safe being at Croatoan, which is the place where Manteo was born, and the savages of the island our friends."*

Before he could reach Croatoan Island to search for them, disaster struck again in the form of another storm which almost grounded the *Hopewell*, and she lost all but one anchor as the two ships tried to reach Croatoan Island. The weather was so foul that the captain of the *Hopewell* and John White agreed to sail south to the Caribbean to get fresh water and make repairs before returning in the spring to search for the colonists. The crew of the *Moonlight* decided to sail back to England with their acting captain. The *Hopewell* never made it to the Caribbean. The storm winds were so strong and adverse that the ship was pushed farther and farther out into the Atlantic, until the captain and White decided to head for the Azores and possibly undertake another supply voyage to Croatoan in the spring. That was not to be. Their plans fell apart in England, and John White finally gave up hope of ever searching for his colonists. From what he had found on Roanoke Island, he was satisfied that they were well and with Manteo's people.

POINT: When John White sailed to England for supplies and additional "planters" for the Roanoke colony, neither he nor the colonists were aware of the seriousness of political events erupting in Europe. John White's resupply of his colony was delayed by the preparations for war with Spain. When England managed to defeat the Spanish Armada, other events and misfortunes prevented John White from returning to his colony for three years. At that late date, circumstances seemed to conspire against him, and he was not able to make a thorough search for his colonists. He did find hard evidence that they had relocated to Croatoan Island, but he was unable to search there before returning to England. He was certain his colonists were alive and well and that they had followed a prearranged plan and gone to Croatoan Island where Manteo and his people lived.

The Colonists Were On Their Own

The colonists left no report to describe how they fared when John White did not return as expected, but a careful examination of the facts we know, the disposition of the natives, the geography of the country, reports of explorers at the time and thereafter, as well as the oral tradition of the Indians provide enough evidence for reasonable conclusions.

Some historians have a certain intellectual arrogance about the value of oral tradition, but for centuries oral tradition has been considered a valuable resource. Among cultures with no written history, passing along their oral traditions is an obligation that is taken seriously. Regarding the Lumbee Indians of Robeson County, N.C. in particular, historian Hamilton McMillan wrote, *"Tradition is an Indian's history. Nomadic in their habits they leave no record of their existence, save camping places, and rude pottery in places where they temporarily dwelt."*

Since historians are willing to accept reports and letters written years after an event, when the passage of time dims memories and corrupts details, they should be willing to consider the value of oral tradition as well. Therefore, the authors will give the oral tradition of the Indians consideration in searching for the Lost Colony.

We know from Ralph Lane's reports of the Second Voyage that a fort was constructed on the northeastern end of the island and that houses similar to English thatched-roof cottages of the period were constructed near the fort. We learn from Richard Haklyut's *Discourse of Western Planting* that Sir Walter Raleigh expected any voyage of colonization to include men trained in a wide variety of skills and crafts valuable for starting a new society from scratch. Therefore, when the colonists of the 1587 voyage were put ashore unexpectedly on Roanoke Island, they had skilled craftsmen with them who immediately led them in cleaning and repairing the cottages previously built and even in starting construction of additional dwellings. They came prepared not only to survive, but to thrive in their new homeland. The fort had been razed, but there were enough cottages standing to provide the colonists shelter in the summer weather until the additional houses were completed. No archeological evidence of these houses has been found, but they were constructed toward the northern tip of the island. Any remains of these structures have been obliterated by hundreds of years of erosion from rough seas and high winds.

Unfortunately, the pilot on their voyage, Simon Fernando set a meandering pace through the West Indies, causing the colonists to miss the planting season in Virginia. Fernando had not allowed them to take on the additional supplies they expected to in the West Indies, so the colonists knew immediately that their supplies were inadequate to sustain them for the year it would take to harvest their first crops.

When Ralph Lane's party hastily departed Roanoke Island the previous year, it is likely they left behind some tools and materials which may have been useful to the colonists of 1587. Ralph Lane's party was near to starvation when Sir Walter Drake rescued them. His attempt to provision the colony was prevented by a terrible storm, so it is unlikely they left behind any significant amount of food. If some of the food Drake promised to leave Lane survived the chaos of the storm, the natives would have recovered it as soon as the ships left. Grenville later arrived at the site of Lane's deserted colony and left fifteen men with supplies for two years to hold the territory. Those men disappeared, and any food they had would have been collected by the natives. John White made no mention in his writings of finding any food at the fort. If there had been any sizeable amount of food left behind, White's departure to England for supplies would not have been so urgent.

To make matters worse, there is evidence that the east coast was experiencing a severe drought, and the natural food sources of the region were reduced. Common sense would compel the colonists to ration carefully what supplies they had and supplement them by fishing, hunting, gathering berries, grapes, nuts, and perhaps trading with the friendly Croatoan Indians for whatever they could spare.

It seems probable that they had sufficient supplies to survive at least through the winter. Otherwise, John White would not have sailed away, leaving his daughter and newborn grand-daughter without enough food to survive until he could return to replenish their supplies in the spring. If he had any doubt, he most certainly would have taken them back to England with him.

The fact that the colonists were planning to arrive in Virginia in time to plant crops to store for winter is convincing evidence that they did not starve to death. They came prepared to plant crops and supply their own food. No doubt they brought plenty of seeds with them for the crops they intended to grow on the five hundred acres of land which had been promised to the head of each household. Even if drought along the eastern part of North America had decreased the available food supply, the colonists were already prepared to move inland when John White left them. Surely they would not have remained in a location where conditions prevented planting and harvesting successful crops. It makes no sense that they would remain in one place and starve to death when there was a vast country available to supply their needs. If the members of the Second Voyage did not starve when they depended entirely upon the

Indians to do all of the planting and to supply them with food, then there is no reason to believe that John White's colony of willing workers would have starved.

It was probably not long after John White did not return on schedule that the colonists left Roanoke to move "fifty miles into the maine", as they had been prepared to do before White left for England. The phrase, "fifty miles into the maine", should not be understood to mean fifty miles due west of Roanoke Island. More than likely the colonists, John White and Manteo had discussed several possible locations on the mainland that were suitable for settlement. The most promising locations would have been southwest from Croatoan. The evidence on Roanoke Island and in other locations indicates that though the colonists located first to Croatoan Island, not all of the colonists remained there.

Everything John White found when he returned points to an orderly move, but when? Historical records reveal that the Spanish in Florida had been tipped off about the new colony, but thought it was located in the Chesapeake Bay area. Apparently, someone had leaked the original destination of the voyage, but was unaware of the unexpected change in location. The Spanish governor of St. Augustine sent an expedition north in the summer of 1588 to locate the colony so that he could destroy it. Although the English defeated the

the Spanish Armada in August of 1588, hostilities between the two countries did not cease immediately in the New World, and discovery by the Spanish would have remained a concern for the colonists. When the Spanish ship reached the Chesapeake Bay area, there was no evidence of a colony, and the ship headed south to return to Florida.

Foul weather drove it into the harbor at Port Fernando, where the pilot of the Spanish ship, Vincente Gonzalez, discovered evidence on Roanoke Island that an English colony had been there, but then was deserted. He made no mention of finding any evidence of a massacre or other violence. He surely would have reported such information, since it would have pleased the Spanish governor. Unfortunately, John White was not aware of this information on his return voyage in 1590. It was contained in a secret report to the King of Spain in February, 1600.

From this evidence, it is reasonable to conclude that the colonists left Roanoke Island prior to the summer of 1588. It is possible that they left in small groups with the Croatoan Indians who inhabited the Outer Banks for the spring and summer, hunting and fishing. Before the cold and stormy winter approached, the Indians moved inland. Perhaps these mixed groups of indians and colonists set out at different times.

In his drawings, John White depicts Croatoan villages with approximately ten dwellings. That would be the size group in which the Indians felt comfortable traveling. At least a few men from the colony probably remained on Croatoan Island for a period of time, in case John White should appear. Perhaps those left behind had been given instructions for leading John White to the chosen "seate" of the colonists.

It seems highly unlikely that any of the colonists would have set out into the country without their Indian friends. From the reports of the Second Voyage, it was well known that the Indians were divided into tribes and alliances controlling the various regions of the country. Though all of the contacts with the Indians during the First Voyage had been friendly, the behavior of Sir Richard Grenville, Master Ralph Lane, and his soldiers had divided the Indians into two factions. The larger faction was loyal and friendly to the English, but the other smaller faction viewed them as threatening invaders. Manteo saw the advantages of befriending the English, but Wanchese was convinced they were a danger to his people and no doubt when he returned on the Second Voyage, he advised Wingina to oppose the English. The reader may decide who was the real hero; Manteo who wanted the advantages of an advanced civilization for his people, or Wanchese who was xenophobic and wanted to destroy the English.

John White saw all of this unfolding first hand and undoubtedly passed this information along at least to his assistants in the colony. The colonists were among friends on Croatoan Island, but they would have been aware that it was prudent to travel with friendly natives when venturing into the interior of their new homeland where they had limited understanding of the intricacies of tribal relations. The fact that John White had asked the colonists to leave the symbol of a cross if they were "distressed in any of those places", indicates that he recognized there was the possibility of some "distressing" situation arising. He never specified what particular distress he had in mind, or if he referred to any number of distressing situations that the colonists might face in their new life. More than likely, he was thinking of the danger of the of the Spanish discovering their location, since this was not a garrison of soldiers but a colony.

The Spanish were always a threat to English intrusion in the New World, and Roanoke Island was on the route the Spanish treasure ships followed when returning to Spain. As a matter of fact, Captain Arthur Barlowe of the First Voyage thought the location made it a perfect staging spot for attacks on Spanish ships. It was relatively well hidden, but not impossible to discover.

POINT: The colonists came to Virginia prepared not only to survive, but to establish themselves on large land grants.

Although they arrived too late in the season for planting crops, John White apparently felt they had enough food to survive until at least spring, which would give him enough time for the round trip voyage and time to collect supplies and enlist other "planters". The colonists were in a vast and bountiful country with Indian friends who certainly knew how to survive. There was never any evidence that the colonists perished from starvation, nor did they fall victim to the Spanish. The Spanish had been incorrectly informed that the colonists were at the Chesapeake Bay. When a Spanish ship accidentally came upon the Roanoke fort in the summer of 1588, the colonists had already departed. There was no mention in the Spanish captain's report of evidence of starvation or slaughter. He reported the settlement abandoned. This sets the date of the colonists' departure prior to the summer of 1588.

What About the Indians?

E. Roy Johnson gives a good description of the situation among the Indians in his book, *The Lost Colony in Fact and Legend.* He describes the Croatoans and most other coastal Indians as being of Algonquian stock, while the Indians on the mainland, such as the Neusioks and Corees in the Neuse River area, were Iroquois. The Iroquois-dominated group was led by the powerful Tuscaroras (probably seven or eight tribes) who inhabited the middle reaches of the Roanoke and Neuse rivers and the rich country in between. The other, composed of Algonquian tribes, was led by the Chowanooks of the Chowan River country, northeast of Roanoke River. Several tribes of the Albermarle Sound area, including the Weapomeioks, Roanokes, and it appears, the Croatoans, were members of this alliance.

The Algonquians saw the benefit of befriending the English in the 1580's in order to put the power of their superior weaponry on the Algonquian's side. Ralph Lane's account gives an example of this ploy when he reports that after taking prisoner Menatonon, King of the Chowanooks, that Menatonon suggested an alliance between the English and the Chowanooks. Menatonon's description of the Tuscarora's silver and copper mines so enthralled Lane that he made plans to use Chowanook guides to help him invade Tuscarora territory.

Unfortunately, Chief Wingina set in motion counter measures which resulted in his own death and so unsettled the Indian-English relations that the English abandoned their first colony shortly thereafter.

By the time John White's colony arrived at Roanoke Island in 1587, most of the Indians had followed Menatonon's lead and remained loyal to the English, and only a small group of Wingina's followers had any hostility toward the English. Those attempting to make a second settlement on Roanoke Island would find that the overwhelming majority of Indians in the area were their friends.

There is evidence of a network of ancient Indian trails throughout North Carolina from the coast to the mountains, as well as into what are now the states of Virginia, South Carolina and Georgia. These trails were originally made by animals migrating in search of food and were usually close to a water supply such as a stream, creek, or river. On these narrow foot paths, the Indians probably traveled single file in small groups. Villages were eventually established fifteen to twenty miles apart, or the distance of one day's travel on foot. Years later, colonists used these same trails and widened them as they moved westward across the new land. Many present-day roads and highways have been built over portions of the old Indian trails.

The topography of North Carolina made it difficult for early explorers to penetrate the wilderness away from the shoreline. Most of the rivers run northwest to southeast instead of east and west and are navigable from the coast only as far as the eastern edge of the Piedmont. At that point the rivers often have falls and are fast-flowing with numerous rapids where there is a drop in elevation between the Piedmont and the Coastal regions.

The river banks are usually steep rather than gently sloping, making crossing difficult. While other areas were easily explored using waterways into the west, the interior of North Carolina was protected from exploration longer, because travel had to be on foot. This limited the distance that could be covered in a day, probably not more than fifteen to twenty miles, and also limited the amount of supplies one could carry. This natural feature would prove a blessing to those seeking refuge inland.

It seems plausible that the colonists from Roanoke Island and their Croatoan Indian friends would have used the natural waterways from the coast as far inland as possible. At that point, they could have picked up the established system of Indian trails to complete their relocation inland. A question that remains is why historians and researchers haven't focused more attention on this route. Too many seem satisfied simply to say the colonists disappeared, but that is not a satisfactory conclusion for historians and researchers. Over a hundred people don't just disappear! We may not know where they went, but they went somewhere.

Writing in 1984, noted authority David Beers Quinn wrote in *The Lost Colonists, Their Fortune and Probable Fate* that the Indians were not xenophobic, and a small group of colonists had little to fear as long as they were not hostile to the Indians. In summary, he states, *"The Lost Colony disappeared therefore, into a land already inhabited and developed where they might assimilate or remain separate. Their fate and fortune lay in the hands of the native people."* The records we have indicate these would have been helping hands for friendly colonists wishing to live in peace.

POINT: In spite of any hostilities stirred up with some of the Indians by Ralph Lane and his men in 1585-1586, by the time John White's colony arrived a year later there had been time for the Indians to settle back into their normal alliances and power structures. The majority of the Indians in the Roanoke area remained friendly to the English. When the colonists joined the Croatoan Indians to move inland, the rivers from the coast could take them as far as what is now the Piedmont region of North Carolina. From there, they could travel farther inland by an established network of Indian trails to make their journey easier.

Raleigh's Efforts To Find His Colony

Raleigh's patent from Queen Elizabeth expired if he failed to establish a permanent colony within six years. When it appeared that the colony was lost, Raleigh tried to maintain his patent by acting as though the colonists were still alive in Virginia. He asked privateers to stop by Roanoke to search for them, but privateers were more interested in the riches they could take by raiding treasure ships than in searching for colonists. There is nothing to indicate any of these privateers ever stopped at Roanoke. Raleigh himself never participated in a search for the colonists. The Queen was determined to keep him near her, and he had many other pursuits to keep him occupied, such as overseeing the estates the Queen had granted him in Ireland.

Acting as though his colony were still active, in 1589, Raleigh transferred his interest in his patent to a group of London merchants, but he retained for himself a fifth of all gold and silver that might be discovered.

Finally, in 1602, fifteen years after the Roanoke Island colonists were last seen, Raleigh decided to renew his search for the colonists. According to John Brereton, he sent Samuel Mace, an experienced mariner, *"who had been at Virginia twice before"*. Though the avowed purpose of this venture was to search for the Lost Colony, skeptics have charged that since Raleigh's patent had expired, this effort was nothing more than an attempt to keep it in force by acting as though his Roanoke Island colonists still occupied Virginia soil.

Of course, finding them alive would have been the key to validating his old patent, but as long as Raleigh continued to act as though the colonists were still alive in "Virginia", there was no proof otherwise. In an apparent attempt to prevent Mace and the crew of his small bark from spending their time in privateering activities as previous searchers had done, Raleigh hired them for monthly wages. Mace attempted a direct crossing of the Atlantic, instead of taking the circuitous but more common Caribbean route, and made landfall in the vicinity of Cape Fear rather than Roanoke. He and his men remained there for a month, trading with the natives for roots and herbs, including valuable sassafras. Eventually, they headed north along the coast, but instead of searching for the lost colonists, they returned to England, claiming that the bad weather and loss of some principal equipment prevented them from searching Hatteras, Croatoan Island, or the mainland area of Dasamonguepeuk.

Other events prevented Raleigh from mounting another search even if he had wanted to, but it is interesting that Raleigh never sent anyone to search in the Chesapeake Bay area. If Sir Walter Raleigh or John White had any reason at all to think the colonists had relocated to that area, certainly Raleigh would have directed searchers there.

POINT: Although Sir Walter Raleigh asked privateers and others to search at Roanoke Island for the colonists, there is no evidence that any did so. Raleigh himself never participated in a search. Since no search was ever directed to the Chesapeake Bay area, it is clear that no one had any reason to believe the colonists had moved there.

Things Were Changing In England

At this time in England, political events were making it convenient to perpetuate the idea that Sir Walter Raleigh's colony had disappeared. When Queen Elizabeth I died in 1603, James I became King. James was the son of Mary Queen of Scots, Queen Elizabeth's cousin and enemy. King James already held a grudge against Raleigh for his part in Queen Elizabeth's decision to execute one of the King's favorites, the Earl of Essex, for treason. His hatred of Raleigh didn't seem assuaged by the fact that Essex also had been one of Queen Elizabeth's favorites.

Once he became King, James was particularly unhappy with the very generous benefits Queen Elizabeth had allowed Raleigh in his patent to explore and colonize America. The King wanted all of those riches to fill his treasury instead of

Raleigh's pockets. If the Roanoke Colony could be said to have failed before the six year time limit ran out, Raleigh's patent ended and King James benefitted.

To help matters along, King James had Raleigh charged with treason and sentenced to death in a sham of a trial. If Raleigh were executed for treason, his patent became void. Raleigh's death was postponed, and he languished in prison until he was able to convince King James that he was certain he could secure great riches for the King's treasury if he would allow Raleigh to make a voyage to Guiana.

The King agreed and Raleigh sailed to Guiana where disaster struck. Not only did Raleigh fail to find any riches, but his company managed to engage in battle with the Spanish occupiers in which Raleigh's son was killed. When Raleigh returned to England, his sentence was reinstated and he was executed.

POINT: With the death of Queen Elizabeth I, Raleigh's fortunes diminished. King James would have been only too happy to put to rest any hopes that some of Raleigh's colonists remained alive in Virginia. He wanted Raleigh's patent to expire and finally tried him for treason and imprisoned him. Raleigh was released briefly on the promise that he could gain great riches for King James in the New World, but when he failed the king executed him.

The Reports From Jamestown

The information that has been given the most attention in determining the fate of the Lost Colony came from reports made by members of the Jamestown Colony. The Jamestown Colony wasn't settled until 1607, and by the time those colonists barely survived their first winter and establish the colony enough to send out search parties, it had been twenty years since John White had last seen his colonists.

There are problems with giving the reports from Jamestown too much significance. When the Chesapeake Bay colony was organized, Queen Elizabeth I was dead and King James I was the new monarch. King James saw the potential of having colonies in America, but like most new leaders he preferred to get the credit for success.

It would have suited King James if no survivors of the Lost Colony were ever found, and the Colony named in his honor became the first to succeed. That sentiment could not have been a secret to the leaders of Jamestown. It was an age when being impolitic could mean a death sentence, and pleasing the sovereign was paramount. Even though King James seemingly supported the searches for the Lost Colony sent out from Jamestown, they were so perfunctory that one has to wonder whether the searches were more for compiling a record of effort than for actually finding any colonists.

In the beginning stage of the Jamestown Colony when survival was precarious, advice from experienced survivors of the Roanoke Colony would have been of great benefit. However, as the Jamestown colonists adapted to their new environment and learned to survive on their own, there would have been less and less urgency to find other colonists. Perhaps as the years passed with no contact with survivors of the Roanoke Colony, it was easy to believe they had perished and further searches were useless.

Over the years (1609-1612), several parties were sent out from Jamestown to look for the Roanoke colonists, but none were found. There was a sighting of an elusive savage boy who appeared to have light hair and eyes. One of the leaders of the Jamestown colony, George Percy, describing an expedition into the Virginia interior in May 1607, made the following comment about a discovery at a place thought to have been located on the James River some twenty miles below the falls: *"At Port Cotage in our Voyage up the River, we saw a Savage Boy about the age of ten yeers, which had a head of haire of perfect yellow and a reasonable white skinne, which is a Miracle amongst all Savages."*

For more than a century history sleuths have cited this report as the first bit of evidence that descendants of the lost colonists were living in the area when the Jamestown Colony arrived.

This is slim evidence for settlement by the Roanoke colonists in the Chesapeake Bay area. In addition to an encampment of Englishmen from the Second Voyage being in the area, the natives told of white sailors who had been washed ashore on uninhabited Wocokon Island (present-day Portsmouth Island south of Croatoan Island), and remained for some period of time while they constructed a craft to sail across the sea. The craft broke apart and washed ashore, but the sailors apparently perished. It's not likely that these were the only sailors washed ashore over the years at other locations along the coast, as the coast of North America was on the route of ships returning from the Americas to Europe. The natives also mentioned trading with white men in the past, and some historical records indicate that the Spanish may have explored in the area prior to the arrival of the English. There are a number of possible explanations for a light-haired boy being seen among the Indians. Therefore, the sighting of a mixed-blood child proves nothing conclusive regarding the Roanoke colonists.

Captain John Smith, President of the Jamestown Colony, made several references to the lost colonists in his book, *A True Relation-Of Such Occurances and Accidents of Naote as Hath Hapned in Virginia Since the First Planting of that Collony.* In his account of a meeting with the King of the Pamunkey Indians, he said, *"What he knew of the dominions he spared not to acquaint me with, as of certain men clothed at a place called Ocanahonan, clothed like me."* Later, in his travels into the interior at a place called Weramocomoco, the local Indian chief, or "Emperour" as Smith described him, gave still more information.

"Many Kindomes hee described mee… The people cloathed at Ocamahowan, he also confirmed; and the Southerly Countries also, as the rest that reported us to be within a day and a halfe of Mangoge, two dayes of Chawwonock, 6. From Roonock, to the south part of the backe sea: He described a countrie called Anone, where they have abundance of Brasse, and houses walled as ours." Smith's interest was sufficiently whetted either by the mention of abundant brass or by the possibility of finding some of the lost colonists for him to send a delegation in search of the people who dressed like the English and lived in English-style houses, with the following results: *"We had agreed with the King of Paspahegh, to conduct two of our men to a place called Panawicke beyond Roonok, where he reported many men to be appareled. Wee landed him at Warraskoyack, where playing the villaine and deluding and for rewards, returned within three or four days after, without going further."*

This failed attempt to make contact with the supposed lost colonists was mentioned again in a 1610 report prepared by the governors and councilors of the Jamestown Colony.

"If with these we compare the advantages which we have gotten, in the shortness and security of the passage, in the intelligence of some of our Nation planted by Sir Walter Raleigh, yet alive, within fifty mile of our fort, we can open the womb and bowels of this country; as is testified by two of our colony sent out to seek them, who, (though denied by the savages speech with them), found crosses and Letters the Characters and assured Testimonies of Christians newly cut in the barks of trees."

It has proven difficult for historians to identify these places mentioned by Smith. There was little consistency in spelling among writers of this period. Referring to the same location, Smith used these various spellings: "Ocanahonan", "Ocamahowan", Ocanahawan" and "Ochanahoen". John Smith may not have been the best speller, but he was a talented cartographer, mapping Virginia from his own explorations and from reports of others. He sent this map to England in 1608, with three notations pertinent to the mystery of the Lost Colony. In what is now North Carolina, he marked an area some believe is on the Neuse or Tar Rivers, but according to John White's map and other reports is more likely on the Chowan River. Smith indicated: *"Here remayneth 4 men clothed that came from Roonock to Ocanahawan."* In an area north and west of that site Smith wrote: *"Here the King of Paspahege reported our men to be and wants to go."* The third notation is in the James River area: *"Here Paspahege and 2 of our own men landed at Pananiock."*

Instructions sent from England in May, 1609, by the council of the Virginia Company to the Governor of Jamestown seem to support the indirect references to the lost colonists by George Percy and John Smith. It was their suggestion to establish a "principall and chiefe seate" for the Jamestown Colony near *"a towne called Ohonahorn seated where the River of Choanock devideth it self into three branches and falleth into the sea of Rawnocke"*. It is generally accepted that this site was on the west side of the Chowan River (Bertie County, North Carolina).

The council further advised: *"besides you are neere to Riche Cooper mines of Titanoc and may passé them by one braunche of this River and by another Peccarecamicke where you shall finde foure of the englishe alive, left by Sir Walter Rawley which escaped from the slaughter of Powhatan of Roanocke, uppon the first arrival of our Colonie, and live under the proteccon of a wiroane called Gespanocon, enemy to Powahatan, by whose consent you shall never recover them."*

William Strachey served as secretary of the Jamestown Colony for several years, and when he returned to England he wrote a report that referenced the Lost Colony. *"At Peccarecanick, and Ochanahoen, by the Relation of Machumps, the People have howses built with stone walls, and one story above another, so taught them by those English who escaped the slaughter at Roanoak.... At Ritanoe, the Weroance Eyanoco preserved 7. Of the English alive, fower men, twoo Boyes, and one young Maid, (who escaped and fled up the River of Chanoke) to beat his Copper, of which he hath certayn Mynes at the said Ritanoe."* (The Historie of Travell Into Virginia Britania). Referring to the area along the Atlantic coast south of Chesapeake Bay to Florida, Strachey wrote: *"In this Country it was that Sir Walter Raleigh planted his two Colonies, in the Island foresaid called Roanoak."*

He also wrote of Chief Powhatan: *"he doth often send unto us to temporize with us, awayting perhapps but a fitt opportunity (inflamed by his bloudy and furious priests) to offer us a tast of the same Cuppe which he made our poore Countrymen drinck off at Roanoak."*

There are those who adhere to the theory, based on the supposed declaration of Chief Powhatan, that he massacred all of the Roanoke colonists. David Beers Quinn writes that when William Strachey used the terms "at Roanoke" and "of Roanoke" in the writings he completed in 1612, he was not referring to Roanoke Island, but to the settlers from the Roanoke Colony who possibly moved to the Chesapeake area. Powhatan did attack and wipe out the Chesapeake

Indians in 1607, because they refused to assimilate into his expanding confederacy of tribes. If one believes that any of the Roanoke colonists were living with the Chesapeakes, then they would have suffered the same fate.

Powhatan's confession reportedly was made to John Smith in December, 1608, twenty years after the lost colonists were last seen. It is inconceivable that a man with Smith's experience would not have realized the importance of such a confession and the necessity of having reliable witnesses to hear it with him. Yet there were no witnesses to the supposed confession. Smith served for a time as governor of the Jamestown Colony, but inexplicably did not mention that important confession in any of his writings or to anyone else for fifteen years, until it appeared in a 1623 book, **Hakluytus Posthamus**, by Samuel Purchas.

There seems to be no doubt that this information came directly from John Smith, who was cooperating closely with Purchase in collecting material for the book. Such a long silence about a critical piece of information, along with Smith's reputation for manipulating and embellishing facts and for being a dramatic story teller and self-promoter, puts his report of Powhatan's confession in the category of a good story, but does not give it validity as evidence.

This supposed confession raises the question of why Powhatan would not have massacred the Jamestown colonists as well, especially since they were at times greatly reduced in numbers and weakened from starvation. He certainly had the power to do it. Apparently, he had expanded his territory about that time and controlled an estimated nine-thousand people. If John Smith believed Powhatan's confession, why were any more searches for the colonists made from Jamestown after 1608? The confession may have been John Smith's way of appeasing the king and saving his reputation after so many years of failure to locate any of the Roanoke colonists.

One explanation suggested to explain John Smith's long delay in revealing Powhatan's supposed confession is that by the time Powhatan made his confession, the English had already bestowed honors upon him in acts of friendship. It would have been embarrassing to reveal that they had honored the man who slaughtered the colonists of Roanoke. There is another possible explanation for Smith's story of Powhatan's confession. When he learned that the explorers sent to the area of the Chowan River did not make contact with any Englishmen, he knew there was no one to contradict any story he told. Perhaps the massacre story was intended to put fear in the hearts of his struggling colonists of the fate they would suffer if they gave up their struggle.

There are at least four major problems with Powhatan's confession. First, the slaughter was reported to have taken place shortly before the arrival of the Jamestown Colony, which meant the colonists would have been living peacefully with the natives for twenty years when Powhatan suddenly decided to slaughter them for no particular reason.

Second, we know from Spanish reports that they found the Roanoke colony abandoned in 1588, and John White found it so in 1590. Therefore, there were no colonists at Roanoke for Powhatan to slaughter.

Third, there is no archaeological evidence to validate a massacre of colonists in the Jamestown or the Roanoke areas.

Fourth, the reports from the Jamestown Colony don't support Powhatan's confession. Explorers from Jamestown reported learning of some Roanoke colonists who escaped the slaughter held captive by at least one Indian ruler, Chief Eyanco, forcing the English to work in his copper mines.

In another location they reported Indians living in houses constructed of stone as shown them by the English. They were also reported to have tame turkeys when the Indians did not have domesticated fowl. The key question is how is it possible that skills which require long periods of time to acquire, such as constructing stone houses and domesticating fowl, could have been taught to the Indians by the English who escaped the slaughter. The supposed time of the slaughter was just prior to the arrival of the Jamestown colony. Therefore, it would have been impossible for any survivors to teach the natives such skills before the Jamestown colonists reported these events.

There is the slight possibility that Powhatan could have killed any colonists left behind on Croatoan Island to wait for John White's return after the main body of colonists left the island, but those would have been very few in number and certainly not amounting to a "massacre". These few colonists would have been out of Powhatan's immediate territory and absolutely no threat to him, so one has to wonder why he would bother. Further diminishing Powhatan's claim is the fact that he would not have known how many English were living on Roanoke Island.

In order to reach them, he would have needed canoes for all of his war party. It is inconceivable that his warriors would have carried so many canoes through the Great Dismal Swamp. Another complication to such an attack was that he would have had to pass through King Menatonon's territory for a great distance, and it is not likely that Menatonon would have allowed that.

When John Lawson visited Croatoan Island (Hatteras Island) in the early 1700's, the Indians readily told him with pride that their ancestors were white men. In his talks with them, they never mentioned any massacre of their ancestors by Powhatan. No one else who visited the island before or after Lawson reported any information about a massacre of white men on that island. If there had been a massacre, it would have been a significant piece of information which the Indians surely would have shared. In his book, **Sir Walter Raleigh's Lost Colony**, Hamilton McMillan writes, *"If we accept their traditions, they held communication with the coast of North Carolina long after the exodus of the colonists, and it is not improbable that it was a party of this tribe which Lawson describes in 1714 as visiting their old hunting grounds and who described their ancestors as people who would "talk in a book."* They were descendants of the Lost Colony.

Adherents to the massacre theory point to the "proof" which Chief Powhatan presented: a musket barrel, some iron pieces, and a bronze mortar.

This account is found in Samuel Purchas' book, **Pilgrimes** (1625). These items are not convincing evidence of a massacre, and their source is unclear. The obvious questions for an impartial researcher is why Powhatan did not keep the whole musket, which would have been a great prize, instead of just the barrel? Was the musket barrel definitely identified as English, or was it possibly Spanish? If it were English, did it come from Ralph Lane's encampment?

And why not take something useful from a massacre like an ax, a sword, a knife, or the personal possessions of the English instead of just some pieces of iron. All of the items Powhatan presented seem more like items obtained by scavenging deserted English encampments. We know that on the Second Voyage Ralph Lane and a party of men explored in the Chesapeake Bay area and encamped there. They were also encamped in the Roanoke Island area for a year before they left. It is possible that Powhatan traded with other Indians who scavenged a deserted campsite, or even traded with Englishmen himself for these items. They certainly are not proof of a massacre. Chief Powhatan was a powerful leader and no fool. He must have been concerned about what threat the English would be to his authority. Once he realized that no one knew what happened to the Roanoke Colonists, it seems logical that he seized that opportunity to enhance his stature as a strong and dangerous leader by claiming that he massacred the colonists.

Although no evidence of a slaughter of the Roanoke colonists was ever found, Powhatan's boast apparently had the intended effect of impressing the Jamestown colonists with his power and savagery. Strachey goes on to say, "His Majestie hath bene acquainted that the men, women, and children of the first plantation at Roanoak were by practize and Commandment of Powhatan (he himself perswaded thereunto by his Priests) miserable slaughtered without any offence given him.... By the first planted (who 20. And od years had peaceably lyved and intermixed with those Savadages, and were out of his Territory.)"

Apparently, no one questioned why Powhatan would suddenly massacre colonists who were living peaceably outside his territory for twenty years and presenting no threat to him.

It is time to set the historical record straight. For far too long, Powhatan and those of his nation have born the stigma of murdering the colonists of Roanoke Island. The probability is overwhelming that this perpetuated story as being part of the beginning of "civilized America" is not true. There is no hard evidence to support Powhatan's confession to John Smith of a slaughter at Roanoke, and yet that story continues to appear in history books as credible.

John Smith made yet another reference to the search for the Lost Colony in his "Description of Virginia" published in 1612. *"Southward they went to some parts of Chanwonock and the Mangoages, to search them there left by Sir Walter Raleigh;for those parts of the Towne of Chrisapeake, hath formerly been discovered by M. Harriot and Sir Ralph Layne."*

In other words, the explorers were directed specifically to search in the upper area controlled by King Menatonon.

Why were the searchers directed to that particular area rather than another area? Someone obviously knew of the plans for removal discussed by John White and the colonists before he left them in 1587. The indication is that at least one plan considered by White and the colonists was for some or all of the colonists to move from Roanoke to live among the native friends of the Chowan River area, and those plans were known to the leaders of the Jamestown Colony.

The final clues in the literature of the Jamestown settlement can be found in "The Proceedings of the English Colony in Virginia", a report prepared by several leaders of the colony and published in 1612. The report mentions Captain Smith's dealings with an Indian chief on one of his journeys. *"The Captaine thanked him for his good counsel, yet the better to try his love, desired guides to Chowanoke, where he would sent a present to that king to bind him his friend. To performe this journey was sent Michael Sicklemore, a honest, valiant, and painefull soldier, with him, two guids, and directions how to search for the lost company of Sir Walter Rawley and silke grasse...Mr. Sicklemore well returned from Chawonock, but found little hope and lesse certainetie of them that were left by Sir Walter Rawley."*

The report goes on to describe another search. *"So that Nathanell Powell and Anas Todkill were also, by the Quiyoughquohanocks, conducted to the Mangoages to search them there. But nothing could we learne but they were all dead."* This mention of Michael Sicklemore, Nathanell Powell and Anas Todkill searching into the southern part of Virginia for the Lost Colony is the last reference to Raleigh's planters by the settlers of Jamestown.

Again, this is an indication that someone in Jamestown knew that the Roanoke colonists had planned to move inland, and perhaps they had reason to believe the colonists had relocated to the upper portion of the Chowan River. It is possible that at least some of the colonists went to that location, expecting that eventually a colony would be planted there. Any artifacts found to suggest English presence would not necessarily prove that the Roanoke colonists were there, since Ralph Lane explored this area on the Second Voyage and could have left behind some artifacts.

The chain of evidence in the mystery does not pick up again for more than forty years, at which time Virginia Dare would have been in her sixties, if still alive.

In reviewing the "reports" and "sightings" coming out of the Jamestown colony, it must be acknowledged that there was no hard, conclusive, or even convincing evidence that the Roanoke colonists moved to the Chesapeake Bay area and lived with the friendly Chesapeake Indians.

The searchers heard tantalizing tales of survivors in various places, but none actually saw or spoke with a survivor of the Roanoke colony. An impartial researcher cannot accept as fact the unsubstantiated reports of writers who possibly had reasons for perpetuating a particular scenario of events. The report that Chief Powhatan massacred the Roanoke Colonists is also unsubstantiated. Perhaps it is best to follow the practice at the time of those in England who knew John Smith best and viewed his writings as entertaining, but not to be taken too seriously.

The authors were unable to cite the first use of the term "Lost Colony" in referring to the colony at Roanoke. Hamilton McMillan used it in his book in 1888, but nowhere did we encounter the colony described as the "Slaughtered Colony" or the "Massacred Colony". Evidently John Smith's story wasn't good enough to be memorialized in the familiar name we know as the "Lost Colony".

Furthermore, in the record of searches made from the Jamestown colony, there is a glaring error of investigation. No one ever visited the actual site of the Lost Colony to look for evidence, or to try to trace the colonists from their last known location. This might be attributed to the fact that Jamestown had enough problems just trying to survive.

However, since locating the Roanoke colonists was one of the orders of the Jamestown Colony, it would have made more sense to go directly to the original site rather than waste time on fruitless searches that amounted to no more than wild goose chases. Granted that after twenty years it might have been difficult to discover any hard evidence of their fate, but failing to explore the original site of the Lost Colony surrendered any traces they left behind to time and the elements. Erosion by wind and water being what it is on the Outer Banks, it is no wonder so little archaeological evidence has been found. Hundreds of feet of shoreline could have washed away since 1587. Since the boundaries of Roanoke Island have changed over time due to wind and waves, it is highly possible that the sands beneath the ocean now conceal any artifacts left behind.

POINT: Reports from the Jamestown Colony have been very influential in creating the popular scenario of a slaughter of the Roanoke colonists. The searches and reports from Jamestown came twenty years after John White last saw his colonists. Queen Elizabeth's successor, King James, had a different attitude toward Sir Walter Raleigh and his colony. He had reason to encourage the belief that all of the colonists were dead. There was one "sighting" and several second-hand stories of colonists from Roanoke living in the Chesapeake Bay area, but there was never any evidence.

The most startling story came from Chief Powhatan, who supposedly confessed to slaughtering the Roanoke colonists. There was never any evidence found to support his story, but John Smith made sure that was the story passed down through history.

From an official Spanish report of the time, we know the Roanoke colony had been abandoned in 1588, with no mention of signs of a slaughter or any other distress. There was no search for clues made at the actual site on Roanoke Island or Croatoan Island.

Clues from the Lost Colony

It is difficult to understand why the hard evidence the lost colonists purposely left behind on Roanoke Island is given so little credence. The prearranged message left by the colonists is clear evidence that should be accepted at face value. They did what they promised to do. They left a written message giving their destination when they left Roanoke Island. They moved to Croatoan Island (now known as Hatteras Island). There can be no question that was the first step in their journey, regardless of where they finally settled.

There are those who believe that the word "Croatoan" could have referred to the Indian tribe known by that name and not necessarily Croatoan Island. However, the instructions agreed upon between the colonists and John White required that the colonists write the name of their "seate", meaning location.

When John White returned in 1590 and found the message left by the colonists, he said, *"For at my coming away they were prepared to remove from Roanoke fifty miles in the main.*

Therefore at my departure from them in An. 1587, I willed them, that if they should happen to be distressed in any of those places, that then they should carve over the letters or name a cross..."

Without doubt, White was referring to places and not tribes, and his words indicated that more than one location had been considered. It is possible that Manteo and the Croatoans were consulted about the places they would recommend for settlement. If the colonists had already determined before John White left that they definitely planned to relocate to Croatoan Island, there would have been no need to leave any message at all.

It has also been suggested that "Croatoan" may not have been as clearly a defined location as we assume today. Some maps show it as an island south of Roanoke Island, while other maps show it including part of the mainland. (Ogilby Map of 1672, John Lawsons map of 1709, Mosely Map of 1733, Mouzon Map of 1775, and Price Strother Map of 1808) But what did John White's map show? That, of course, would be the best indication of what he and the Roanoke colonists meant. His map showed Croatoan as a specific Island south of Roanoke Island and not a large general area.

In the publication, **Explorations, Descriptions, and Attempted Settlements of Carolina**, 1584-1590 (State Dept. of Archives and History, Raleigh, N.C. 1953), the original reports of the voyages make clear that Croatoan was definitely a particular island. One reference from the Fourth Voyage states: *"On the 30th of July, Master Stafford and twenty of our men passed by water to the island of Croatoan, with Manteo, who had his mother and many of his kindred dwelling in that island, of whom we hoped to understand some news of our fifteen men, but especially to learn the disposition of the people of the country towards us, and to renew our old friendship with them."*

There is no question from this statement that Croatoan was an island. This quote reveals other important facts as well. The use of the phrase, *"many of his kindred dwelling in that island"*, reveals that many but not all of Manteo's people were living on Croatoan Island. Others of his people were living elsewhere. Also, Master Stafford, who had been on the previous voyage and knew the Indians well, was going not only to renew old friendships, but to ascertain the disposition of all of the Indians toward the English after their absence. This information would have been relayed to John White and the other assistants and would have influenced John White's decision to leave his daughter and baby granddaughter while he returned to England for supplies.

Some historians believe the Roanoke colonists traveled northward to their original destination in the Chesapeake Bay area and may have left behind a small party to wait for John

White's return. They point to the fact that the colonists were left with a small pinnace and possibly a couple of other smaller boats which they could have used to travel to the Chesapeake Bay. This seems highly unlikely. A study of a map of North Carolina and Virginia shows immediately that there was not a favorable route by sea or by land. At the time, there was no waterway directly connecting Roanoke and the Chesapeake Bay, and the boats the colonists had were not made for sailing in the open, treacherous waters of the "Graveyard of the Atlantic", with its unpredictable and violent storms. Furthermore, the small boats could not have transported one hundred and eighteen colonists with supplies and possessions.

The other alternative overland was no more likely. The Great Dismal Swamp lay in their way. Most of the swamp was covered in water. Shortly after 1700, a surveying party led by Col. William Byrd was plotting the dividing line between North Carolina and Virginia. Col. Byrd described pushing through places where the water was neck deep. Water was not the only problem in the swamp. It was full of bears, poisonous snakes and other beasts. Even today it is considered a dangerous place. It is hard to imagine how a group numbering more than one hundred men, women and children could have made it through such terrain and over such a long distance.

When Ralph Lane and his men traveled to the area of the Chesapians during their exploration on the Second Voyage, the trip was arduous for seasoned explorers. Lane listed the distance as one hundred thirty miles. At that point they were instructed by an Indian chief to travel another week to the Chesapeake Bay. There were those among the colonists who had been on the Second Voyage and would have known the rigors of such a venture. The Cheapeake Bay area was not a place visited by the Croatoans, and it seems reasonable that the colonists would want to remain with their friends, the Croatoans, rather than separate and set off on their own into unfamiliar territory.

The fact that the colonists carved "Croatoan" and not "Chesapeake" on the post of the fort undermines the theory that the colony relocated to the Chesapeake Bay. It would make no sense to travel south to Croatoan Island with all of their possessions if their destination was really Chesapeake Bay to the north.

When the colonists moved to Croatoan Island, it is almost certain they did not plan to remain there. Croatoan would not have been a suitable place for a permanent settlement for the same reasons that Roanoke Island was not suitable. Also, with over a hundred additional people living on Croatoan Island, the resources to sustain them would have been overtaxed, especially if drought conditions had diminished the normal food supply. The Indians typically did not stay all year in one location. They occupied the narrow Croatoan Island as a hunting and fishing ground when it suited them, but itseems certain that they had another home inland. When they left Croatoan Island to move inland, the colonists would have followed.

It seems most practical that the colonists and the Indians split into several smaller groups to travel, with the Indians acting as guides, and perhaps even following different routes to their final destination. The groups may have departed Croatoan Island at different times.

Since the Indians moved inland on a regular basis, it may be assumed that they had traditional dwelling places inland. The Croatoan Indians would have known the best route by the waterways and overland trails.

A small group of colonists, more than likely single men, might have remained on Croatoan Island to wait for John White's return. Those staying behind were surely given directions to the new location so they could follow later. Perhaps a few did decide to try to get to the Chesapeake Bay, just in case word of their location at Roanoke had not reached Sir Walter Raleigh and supply ships expected to find them in the Chesapeake Bay area.

There are those who believe that the colonists split into small groups and moved to various strategic locations near the coast, hoping for a better chance of being found by returning

Englishmen. When their hopes were dashed, they regrouped and moved westward many miles inland, settling in an area in southeastern North Carolina.

It is likely that the colonists with their Indian guides followed the Neuse River or the Pamlico River, using their small boats to transport their belongings inland. There was a slipway constructed on Roanoke Island by the English of the Second Voyage, which the colonists could have used to construct additional small boats or rafts if needed to transport their goods into the interior by river.

The Pamlico River may have had the greater attraction to the Croatoan Indians and the colonists if we may judge by Captain Arthur Barlowe's report from the First Voyage as described in the book, **Roanoke Island, The Beginnings of English America** (David Stick, 1983). *"According to his information the area under the domain of Wingina extended a considerable distance from Roanoke Island, especially to the southwest, where the largest of the Wingandacoa settlements was located. This was the village of Secotan, near the shores of the Pamlico River."* This would coincide with the 1888 report of the aged Lumbee Indian woman given to historian Hamilton McMillan that her *"fathers"* came from *"Roanoke in Virginia"*. When inquiry was made regarding the exodus of John White's colony, she stated that the colonists from the Roanoke Colony *"were carried to a settlement on the Neuse*

River by a chief named Wyonoke, who conducted them by land, as they could not be safely conveyed by water across Pamlico Sound in the frail boats of the Indians. She further stated that the English gradually moved westward."

As far as can be determined from Lumbee Indian tradition, the term "Virginia" embraced all of the area adjacent to Pamlico Sound. McMillan then explains that the chief's name, Wyonoke, is likely the same chief mentioned as "Eyanoko" in other places.

At some point along any river they chose, it would have been necessary for them to leave the river and follow the traditional Indian trails in search of a secluded place safe from discovery by the Spanish and suitable for a mixed group of people to establish themselves to begin the new lives they envisioned. The territory of southeastern North Carolina some two hundred or so miles south and west of Pamlico Sound was perfect in this regard, as it remained largely unexplored for the next one hundred years after the attempted settlement on Roanoke Island.

Upon his return to Roanoke Island in 1590, John White was not upset at what he found. To the contrary, he took comfort in the evidence of an unhurried move to a stated location he knew to be safe. Before he left the colonists in 1587, they had agreed that it would be necessary to move off Roanoke

Island at some point. It was not the ideal location to plant a colony given the size of the island, the frequent storms, the treacherous waters, and the chance of being discovered by the Spanish whose treasure ships sailed those waters regularly on return trips to Spain.

When White saw the message the colonists left him and the condition of their settlement, which indicated an orderly departure, he had no question that the colonists were safe on Croatoan Island. When his attempts to visit them on Croatoan Island were thwarted, he did not despair at the fate of his daughter and granddaughter, but simply entrusted them to the Almighty. Naturally, he was anguished over his failure to follow them, but he never indicated that he believed they had perished.

POINT: By prearranged plan before John White departed for England, the colonists left behind a written message at their dwelling place on Roanoke Island that they had gone to Croatoan Island. John White accepted that message when he returned to search for them in 1590. The map he drew of the area and the report of the Fourth Voyage both indicate that "Croatoan" was a particular Island and not a general area. Although the colonists went to Croatoan Island, they did not remain there. They traveled inland with their Indian friends. There is oral tradition among the Lumbee Indians of the Roanoke colonists being conveyed by an Indian chief to a settlement on the Neuse River, and that they later moved westward. The unexplored territory of southeastern North Carolina was a perfect refuge from discovery by the Spanish and a secluded place to begin their new lives.

The geography of the area surrounding Roanoke Island made it unlikely that the colonists traveled north to the Chesapeake Bay. John White was aware of the disposition of the Indians toward the English before he made the decision in 1587 to return to England for supplies. It is certain he would not have left his family in danger.

Reports from Later Explorers

In 1663, a group of Englishmen from Barbados, West Indies under the command of William Hilton explored the Cape Fear River in North Carolina for about a month during the fall. They encountered Indians with a somewhat different culture than the Native Americans met by colonists during the voyages of 1584-1590. These Indians had definitely had prior contact with English speaking people.

The Cape Fear River flows into the Atlantic Ocean at the present town of Southport. Approximately twenty miles from the coast at the city of Wilmington, the river divides into two branches. The river that flows from the east is known as the North East Cape Fear, but the explorers called it the Main River. The river flowing from the northwest was called Hilton's River.

The men first explored the Main River. They traveled upstream a great distance until it became so narrow that fallen trees blocked their passage. During their exploration they did not make contact with any natives nor find any signs of habitation.

In his book, **A New Voyage to Carolina**, John Lawson describes their exploration of the Hilton River. The men came upon four Indians in a canoe who showed no fear of them and sold them baskets of acorns. One of the Indians then followed the explorers' boat from the shore, and from a high bank he shot an arrow into the side of their boat. This behavior was uncharacteristic from what previous explorers had encountered, and the men in the boat were surprised and alarmed.

It is unlikely that the Indian intended to harm the explorers, since the Indians were expert in the use of the bow and arrow. Maybe he was trying to impress the explorers with his skill. His action showed a much more independent nature than the Indians encountered on the First Voyage sponsored by Sir Walter Raleigh. Reports from the First Voyage described the Indians as customarily welcoming newcomers and subservient to their chief in all of their actions. Fortunately, this was true of the other Indians they encountered on their exploration.

Perhaps the independence displayed by this one particular Indian reflected an earlier association of his family with Englishmen moving inland.

When the explorers came ashore to find the Indian who shot the arrow, he had disappeared. They heard singing in the woods, which they took as a challenge to fight, but before they could respond to the challenge they heard two guns go off where they had left their boat with the rest of their party.

When they rushed back to the boat, they were told that an Indian had been creeping along the bank as though he intended to shoot at them again. The men had fired their guns at the Indian, but didn't think they had harmed him, since he quickly ran away. Just then, two other Indians approached them crying, *"Bonny, bonny"*. This was a term which meant "good, pretty, pleasing" to the English, and the Indians apparently associated it with "friendship" in this instance. The explorers confiscated their bows and arrows in exchange for some pretty beads. When the explorers showed the Indians the arrow head still in the side of their boat, they appeared quite concerned and indicated by signs that they knew nothing about it, so the explorers let them go. The use of the word "bonny" indicates that these natives had been in contact and on good terms with the English. Since there is evidence that at least some of the colonists from Roanoke traveled along the Cape Fear River, the Indians may have learned the greeting of friendship from them, which they then expressed to the explorers.

Another indication that these Indians had been in contact with white men at some point in their history was the fact that unlike the natives encountered on the First Voyage who were frightened by gunfire, these Indians showed no fear when the explorers discharged their weapons.

This incident took place near the location that authors McMillan and Lowery called Indian Wells. They describe it as a place where the English of the Lost Colony and the Hatteras Indians dwelt for a period of time. Early maps show the location as being on the northwest branch of the Cape Fear River near the town of East Arcadia. The Price-Strother map of 1808 records the place as "Indian Wells". In his book, **The Story of Fayetteville**, author John Oates lists the distance as being forty-one miles upstream from Wilmington.

As they returned down the river, they spotted the canoe of the Indian who shot at them. When they went ashore, a small group of Indians ran away. The explorers smashed the canoe, tore down the Indian's hut and broke his pots and utensils before they continued their trip down river. Since they seemed to have no trouble identifying his hut and no mention is made of a village, it appears this Indian's hut was standing alone. This was not typical of Indian dwellings, which were arranged in groups for communal living and mutual convenience and often enclosed by strong upright poles or logs for protection. (This is quite different from the Lumbee Indians when they were later discovered living along the Lumber River. They were described as "living in the manner of the Europeans".) The Indian in this instance must have learned the custom of individual living from his people's contact with white men.

Traveling on, the explorers came upon more Indians who cried out "Bonny, bonny" as the others did, but in a display of intimidation the explorers brandished their guns and refused to come ashore. To the explorers' surprise, the Indians seemed not to fear the guns as did the natives encountered on the early voyages, and they seemed to know they would not be harmed as long as they behaved themselves.

The indication here was that these Indians were accustomed to the firing of guns by the English, and this would support a connection with those from the Lost Colony as they traveled inland. Two Indians paddled out and took hold of the explorers' boat, telling them it was "bonny" on shore. Finally, the explorers agreed to go ashore, where about forty men came forward saying, "Bonny". The explorers showed the Indian chief the arrowhead in their boat and pieces of the canoe they destroyed. The chief made a long speech and threw beads into their boat as a sign of great love and friendship, telling them that when he heard of the incident it made him cry. He said he and his men had come to make peace, and that they would tie the arms of the fellow who had wronged them and cut off his head.

This response from the chief is interesting in two respects. The traditional method of execution used by Indians was burning at the stake or bashing in the skull. Beheading was first witnessed by Indians in the Roanoke area at the time of the Second Voyage when Master Ralph Lane's man beheaded the hostile King Pemisapan (Wingina) during a skirmish which followed Lane's attack on Pemisapan's village. Yet somehow these Indians far inland had knowledge of beheading as a form of punishment peculiar to the English. This gives weight to the idea that they had been in contact with the English and were familiar with this English method of punishment.

To make amends, the chief and the explorers exchanged gifts, and the chief offered the explorers two young Indian women who immediately got into their boat. The young women seemed to consider going with the explorers to be a great honor, and it took much convincing to get the women back on shore. It is possible these women were daughters of the chief, and this was further proof of the friendship the Indians extended to white men.

Whatever the reason for one Indian shooting an arrow into the explorers' boat, every other Indian expressed only friendship towards them and wanted to make sure they parted on good terms. It is not unreasonable to assume that these explorers were the beneficiaries of the relationship of friendship and mutual respect that existed between the Indians and the lost colonists when they had been in the area. The explorers named the place Mount Bonny before continuing down the river to return to Barbados.

In 1700, an Englishman named John Lawson had completed his formal education and was seeking to expand his knowledge with travel. Intrigued by what he heard of America, he sailed from England to Charleston in what is now South Carolina. In December of that year, the Lords Proprietors of the colony asked him to make a reconnaissance survey of the interior of Carolina. This was an unexplored area which had not been adequately mapped, and little was known about the natives in the area or their attitude toward the English. Lawson began his journey on December 28, 1700. His party included five other Englishmen, three Indians, and the Indian wife of the guide. They traveled west by canoe toward the mouth of the Santee River, exploring the Wateree River and passing into what is now North Carolina. From there they followed the famous overland "Trading Path" to the northeast to the present day locations of Charlotte, Concord, and Salisbury. They continued on to the Yadkin River, Sapona River and the Rocky River near Lexington. Near the present town of Hillsborough, North Carolina, Lawson met an Indian named Enoe Will, who was willing to act as his guide to the English settlements on the coast. On this trip Lawson and his party were welcomed by the Indians they encountered, and Lawson was able to gain a great deal of information about the various

Indian tribes and their cultures, as well as a good knowledge of the territory.

In the course of the journey, members of the party left for various reasons, until in the end only Lawson, another party member, and his devoted Indian guide, Enoe Will, and a few of his friends ended the journey at Richard Smith's plantation on the Pamlico River.

John Lawson was a surveyor and was for some period of time the Surveyor General of the Carolinas. He was also the co-founder of North Carolina's oldest town, Bath, where he drew plans for lots and streets for the town and established a home there. It was probably in Bath where he reported the discovery of artifacts indicating that the Roanoke colonists lived there for some period of time. He describes the discovery in his book, **A New Voyage to Carolina**: *"Amongst the other Subterraneous Matters, that have been discover'd we found in digging of a well that was twenty six feet deep, at the Bottom, there of many large Pieces of the Tulip-Tree, and several other sorts of Wood, some of which were cut and notch'd and some squared, as the Joices of a House are, which appear'd (in the Judgement of all that saw them) to be wrought with Iron Instruments; it seeming impossible for any thing made of Stone, or what they (the Natives) were found to make use of, to cut Wood in that manner. It cannot be augu'd that Wood so cut, might float from some other Continent because Hickory and the Tulip-Tree are spontaneous in America and in no* *other parts, that I could ever learn… the next is, the Earthen Pots that were often found under Ground, and at the Foot of the Banks where Water has wash'd them away. They are for the most part broken in pieces, but we find them of a different sort, in Comparison of those the Indian use at this day, who have no other, ever since the English discover'd America. The Bowels of the Earth cannot have alter'd them since they are thicker, of another Shape, and Composition, and nearly approach to the Urns of the Ancient Romans."*

The timbers uncovered were notched and squared by metal instruments, not by stone implements. In the report of the Fifth Voyage, when Governor John White returned to Roanoke Island and entered the dwelling place of the colonists colonists he had left there in 1587, he stated, *"we found the houses taken down"*, but he makes no mention of any of the wood from the houses being left behind. This deliberate dismantling of the houses certainly indicates that the colonists removed them for use elsewhere. Since it required a great deal of time and labor to fell trees, cut lumber, and then square and notch the planks as was their method of building at that time, it would be practical to take the planks with them for building houses wherever they planned to settle. The planks may have been used to make rafts to transport their goods on the rivers. Also, there was no mention of any household items, furniture, clothing, or equipment left behind. It was obviously an orderly move. There seems little doubt that the prepared wood uncovered in the well as described by John Lawson was the remains of the colonists' houses from Roanoke Island.

The earthen pots found underground and at the water's edge were not of baked clay as the natives made, but were ceramic ware. Lawson described these pots as completely different from native pottery in thickness, shape, composition, and artistry. There is no question that he felt they were of European origin.

It is interesting that Lawson gives the exact depth of the well. When the author asked an elderly gentleman of the town of Bath at what depth one would expect to find water when digging a well, he answered, *"About twenty-six feet."* It appears that the colonists used this well as a place to dispose of any signs of their presence once they left the area. It is likely they took such precautions out of fear of being discovered and followed by the Spanish. Since John Lawson was not the only person to witness these discoveries, his report may be accepted as credible.

John Lawson also visited Hatteras Island in the early 1700's, and encountered Indians who had gray eyes and knew of books, telling him that their ancestors could read books as the English did. He stated that they were, *"them that wear English dress"*. They claimed to be descendants of the Roanoke colonists and had an oral history of Raleigh's ships appearing off the coast in search of the colonists. This seems to support the integration of the Roanoke colonists with the Indians living on Croatoan Island (Hatteras Island) in the time prior to the 1700's. This evidence of the lost colonists integrating with the Indians on Croatoan Island has merit, since none of the explorers prior to the arrival of the Roanoke colonists ever mentioned any such mixed-race people. The time of their appearance would necessarily have been after 1587 and prior to 1700.

Lawson also told of being given chickens by the friendly natives. Domestic fowl were introduced to the North American Continent by the English. This could indicate another connection to the Lost Colony.

Lawson further reported of the Indians living on Hatteras Island: *"These tell us, that several of their Ancestors were white People, and could talk in a Book, as we do; the Truth of which is confirm'd by grey Eyes being found frequently amongst these Indians, and no others. They value themselves extremely for their Affinity to the English, and are ready to do them all friendly Offices."* Perhaps the gray-eyed Indians Lawson described were descendants of the Roanoke colonists remaining behind on Croatoan Island to await John White's return.

Although there are hints in John Lawson's writings that his

early attitude towards the Indians was somewhat as arrogant as he found among other Englishmen, after spending more time observing the Indians he changed his view. It is worth noting his description of the Indians and their interaction with Englishmen:

"First, they are as apt to learn any Handicraft, as any People that the World affords; I will except none; as is seen by their Canoes and Stauking Heads, which they make of themselves; but to my purpose, the Indian Slaves in South Carolina, and elsewhere, make my Argument good. Secondly, we have no disciplin'd Men in Europe, but what have, at one time or other, been branded with Mutiny, and Murmuring against their their Chiefs. These Savages are never found guilty of that great Crime in a Soldier; I challenge all Mankind to tell me of one Instance of it; besides, they never prove Traitors to their Native Country, but rather chuse Death than partake and side with the Enemy. "They naturally possess the Righteous Man's Gift; they are Patient under all Afflictions, and have a great many other Natural Vertues, which I have slightly touch'd throughout the Account of these Savages. They are really better to us, than we are to them; they always give us Victuals at their Quarters, and take care we are arm'd against Hunger and Thirst: We do not so by them (generally speaking) but let them walk by our Doors Hungry, and do not often relieve them. We look upon them with Scorn and Disdain, and think them little better than Beasts in Humane Shape, though it

well examined, we shall find that, for all our Religion and Education, we possess more Moral Deformities, and Evils than these Savages do, or are acquainted withal. We reckon them Slaves in Comparison to us, and Intruders, as oft as they enter our Houses, or hunt near our Dwellings. But if we will admit Reason to be our Guide, she will inform us, that these Indians are the freest People in the World, and so far from being Intruders upon us, that we have abandon'd our own Native Soil, to drive them out, and possess theirs; neither have we any true Balance, in Judging of these poor Heathens because we neither give Allowance for their Natural Disposition, nor the Sylvian Education, and strange Customs, (uncouth to us) they lie under and have ever been train'd up to; these are false Measures for Christians to take, and indeed no Man can be reckon'd a Moralist only, who will not make choice and use, of better Rules to walk and act by: We trade with them, it's true, but to what End? Not to show them the Steps of Vertue, and the Golden Rule, to do as we would be done by. No, we have furnished them with the Vice of Drunkenness, which is the open Road to all others, and daily cheat them in every thing we sell, and esteem it a Gift of Christianity, not to sell to them so cheap as we do to the Christians, as we call our selves. Pray let me know where is there to be found one Sacred Command or Precept of our Master, that counsels us to such Behaviour? Besides, I believe it will not appear, but that all the Wars, which we have had with the Savages, were occasion'd by the unjust Dealings of the Christians towards them. I can name more than a few, which my own Enquiry has given me a right Understanding of, and I am afraid the remainder (if they come to the test) will prove themselves Birds of the same Feather. As we are in Christian Duty bound, so we must act and behave ourselves to these Savages, if we either intend to be serviceable in converting them to the Knowledge of the Gospel, or discharge the Duty which every Man, within the Pale of the Christian Church, is bound to do. Upon this Score, we ought to shew a Tenderness for these Heathens under the weight of Infidelity; let us cherish their good Deeds, and, with Mildness and Clemency, make them sensible and forwarn them of their ill ones; let our Dealings be just to them in every Respect, and shew no ill Example, whereby they may think we advise them to practice that which we will not be conformable to ourselves..." (**A New Voyage to Carolina** by John Lawson, Edited with an Introduction and Notes by Hugh Talmage Lefler, The University of North Carolina Press, Chapel Hill 1967).

Lawson's observations reveal the patient endurance of the Indians even under harsh treatment by the English, and this confirms that the friendly Roanoke Colonists would have been unlikely to attract hostility from the Indians they encountered.

It appears that there were small pockets of renegade Indians still holding a grudge against Grenville and Lane of the Second Voyage for harsh treatment, but the majority of the Indians fit into Lawson's description. Unfortunately for Lawson, his warnings had little effect on the treatment of the Indians by the English, and he was eventually captured and killed by hostile Indians while he was on an expedition.

POINT: Englishmen from Barbados explored the Cape Fear River in 1663, and encountered Indians who showed definite signs of contact with Englishmen. The possibility is that at a previous time, their tribe came in contact with the Roanoke colonists as they made their way inland. The Indians showed friendship to the explorers. In 1700, explorer John Lawson began an expedition into the interior of North Carolina, which until that time was little known. Lawson was treated with friendship by the natives and learned a great deal about the territory as well as the Indians and their customs. In the town of Bath, North Carolina's oldest town, he uncovered artifacts indicating the Roanoke colonists had lived there for some period of time.

Lawson also visited Hattteras Island (Croatoan Island) and found Indians with gray eyes who told him their ancestors could read books. They dressed as the English did. All of this supports the message of the colonists that they moved to Croatoan Island and intermingled with the Indians. Referring to the treatment of the Indians by the English which Lawson observed, he wrote that even under harsh treatment the

Indians exhibited patient endurance. This is another indication that the Roanoke colonists, intermingled with the Indians and treating them as equals, would have had nothing to fear from the Indians on their journey inland.

Modern Accounts

Hamilton McMillan is a recognized authority on the Indians of North Carolina. His research and documentation have been used by the United States Congress as well as the North Carolina Legislature in considering their decisions regarding Indian affairs. It is worthwhile to examine excerpts from his writings when following the Roanoke colonists "into the maine".

"At the coming of white settlers in the early part of the eighteenth century, there was an Indian settlement in Sampson County, North Carolina, and another at 'Indian Wells', on the south bank of the Cape Fear River, in Bladen County. There were other settlements at Fayetteville and Averasboro. The largest settlement was on the Lumber River, and the territory occupied by them embraced a large part of the present county of Robeson. There is abundant evidence that the land lying between the Big Raft and Little Raft swamps was a great camping ground. This tribe, now known as Croatans, occupied the country as far southwest as the Pee Dee, but the principal seat was on the Lumber, extending along the river for twenty miles."

McMillan writes that on occasion immigrants came to the Lumber River from old settlements towards the east. He mentions *"a Rev. Mr. Blair, who was a missionary to the settlements on Pamlico Sound...(who) writes to his patron Lord Weymouth as follows: 'I think it likewise reasonable to give you an account of a great nation of Indians, who live in that government, computed to be no less than 100,000, many of which live among the English, and all as far as I can understand, a very civilized people.'"* The letter was dated 1703.

Although McMillan recognizes that the number of Indians Mr. Blair used is probably an exaggeration and the location of the tribe indefinite, he writes, *"There is reason to believe that the descendants of the lost colonists were living in a region of country southwest of Pamlico at the time in which he (Mr. Blair) writes, and that they emigrated westward to the interior, where a large body of Indians and descendants of the lost Englishmen had previously settled. It is probable that the civilized Indians, mentioned by the missionary, were a portion of the tribe to-day known as Croatans, as there was no other tribe to which the reference could apply. At that early day very little was known of the region to the southwest of Pamlico Sound, and the missionary may have traveled one hundred miles in reaching the place of his labor, which seemed to be a great distance from other precincts visited by him."*

McMillan points out that in 1703 there were no known settlements of white men beyond the area around Pamlico Sound. It was not until 1729 that a settlement was made on a tributary of the Cape Fear River known now as Cross Creek at the present-day town of Fayetteville. McMillan describes the piercing of the wilderness by emigrants: *"At the coming of white settlers there was found located on the waters of the Lumbee, as the Lumber River was then called, a tribe of Indians, speaking English, tilling the soil, owning slaves and practicing many of the arts of civilized life. These Indians called themselves 'Malungeans,' and this name is still retained among the Indians in Butler County, Tennessee, whose ancestors are claimed by the tribe in Robeson County to have come originally with their ancestors from Eastern North Carolina. French emigrants, as early as 1690, had settled on Pamlico Sound, where they came in contact with a mixed race, to whom they gave the name Melange. The descendants of these people were called Melangeans, and the transition from Melange to Malungean was easy... If we credit the traditions of the Croatans in Robeson, the greater part of the tribe had previously moved towards the southwest and were settled at various places along the great trails leading from the mountains to points on the coast."*

A good description of the English speaking Indians the settlers found along the Lumber River is given in the book, **The Only Land I Know – A History of the Lumbee Indians** (Adolph L. Dial and David K. Eliades). *"Clinging fiercely to their Indian origins, the Lumbees nonetheless have no remnants of their Indian language which might provide clues to their relationship* *with other Native Americans. Only traditions and folktales remain as evidence, tales which link this unique group with the lost survivors of the Roanoke Colony as well as with the Eastern band of the Sioux Indians, the powerful and highly assimilated Cherokee, and the Tuscarora Indians."*

In tracing the inland journey of the lost colonists, it is plausible to ask how they found their way. In McMillan's book he writes that the Indians whom the colonists joined were part of the Cherokee Indians who had a great system of trails connecting their principal settlements all the way to the Alleghany Mountains. He details several of the major trails. One extended through Marlboro County in upper South Carolina and through the North Carolina counties of Robeson, Cumberland, Sampson, Duplin, Jones and Craven counties all the way to Roanoke.

This entire trail was known as the Lowery Road, but is now known by that name only in Robeson and Cumberland counties in North Carolina. Another Indian trail extended from the mountains of Buncombe County nearly directly east to join the Lowery Road in Fayetteville, North Carolina.

Two present-day roads in Fayetteville, Morganton Road and Yadkin Road, were originally Indian trails from the mountains to hunting and fishing grounds in Eastern North Carolina. Both trails met up with the great Lowery Road near the mouth of Cross Creek leading to the Cape Fear River. At the old settlement in Sampson County, McMillan found that there was a branch of the great Lowery Road leading to the Cape Fear River at Averasboro. According to indian tradition, this branch of the Lower Road, the "upper road", was used when streams along the main route were too swollen to allow passage. McMillan mentions yet another Indian trail, also called Lowery Road, leading from Fayetteville, North Carolina west through Robeson County across the Lumber River and on through Scotland, Richmond and Anson counties to the mountains.

It was on this road as well as the main Lowery Road that McMillan details evidence of past battles. Numerous mounds were found containing bones of adults whose crania were all *"of Caucasian type and show greater intellectual development than those of savage Indians"*. Particularly well preserved bones were discovered in a mound beside the Lowerie Road at Davis' Bridge in Cumberland County. Many skeletons were buried face downward. The skulls were all Caucasian in type. The bones quickly fell to pieces when exposed to air, indicating they were buried in the distant past.

This is confirmed by the fact that the "Caucasian" skeletons were buried in the traditional Indian style. As all of the remains were found to be Caucasian, perhaps the English bent their rules a bit and exercised some of the Indian rituals and customs. This would have been at a very early date, prior to the Indians accepting the English culture as their own. This could also indicate that each culture preferred to bury their own in separate sites. Two cultures came together and changed some of their traditional customs.

In the area of the Lowery Road, discoveries were made indicating that people with knowledge of various trades and with greater engineering skills and more advanced tools than Indians possessed were in the area prior to the arrival of white emigrants in 1730. According to McMillan, the first settlers arriving in the area of the present town of Hope Mills in Cumberland County found an old dam on Little Rockfish Creek, along with the ruins of a mill for grinding. At the time of McMillan's writing in 1888, the mill rocks were still buried in the sand at the bottom of the stream.

He locates this mill about one mile from the Lowery Road. Another mill site of similar crude construction was located near Pate's Station in Robeson County. It is entirely possible that these were the first water powered grist mills constructed in North America, since the colonists from Roanoke moved inland within five years after 1587. The Jamestown Colony was resupplied, and it is likely they used animals instead of water to power their grinding equipment. It must be remembered that the native Americans encountered by the colonists had no knowledge of the wheel and the many ways it could be used. Their terrain was not suited to the use of wheeled vehicles. Instead, the Indians drug burdens on hides attached between two poles. Neither did they have the tools or technical skill to build a grist mill, but the colonists would have.

An interesting find in the same general area was what he calls, "Indian Walls". He describes the walls as being constructed of red sandstone to an original height of two stories, with the entire structure measuring forty feet by sixty feet. These are the approximate measurements of early churches built at Jamestown, Virginia and Bath, North Carolina. There is no definite proof that this building was a church, but there is Indian tradition indicating that there were once churches at points on the great roads from Roanoke towards the southwest.

According to tradition, one of the churches was close to the Lowery Road near Rockfish Creek in Cumberland County. Hamilton McMillan reported that *"an aged citizen of Cumberland County remembered seeing the walls of this church, known as 'Indian Walls' from 1812 to 1837, when the material was used in building the basement of the Rockfish Cotton Factory"*. The red sandstone was used in the east end of the basement story of the Hope Mills cotton mill.

Even to this day, some of these large old blocks of red sandstone adorn the yards of homes in Hope Mills. The walls had fallen to no more than six or seven feet high before they were removed in 1837. This was very likely the first church built in North America of a more permanent material than wood. The brick church in Jamestown was not constructed until 1639. Such a substantial structure indicates that the people planned to make this a permanent dwelling place and that they retained their custom of religious activity. The dimensions suggest a rather large population. Although red sandstone is abundant in the area, McMillan said that no quarry had been found at the time of his writing where the sandstone was acquired.

McMillan further reports a significant find on the west side of the Cape Fear River just a few miles east of the Lowery Road.

In cutting a canal in 1860 to drain a large swamp in the area, workers discovered a great crossway that led east. There were trees on this crossway whose concentric grains dated the trees at two hundred years old.

The entire area where these ancient structures were found contains much evidence to indicate that thousands of people camped there at various times long ago. However, the Croatans who claim their ancestors occupied this area cannot provide any particular tradition as to who constructed the dam or the sandstone structure.

There were Indians living in Harnett County at the time McMillan was writing who were very expert in the use of the cross-bow *"constructed on the model of the old English cross-bow"*. McMillan describes the bow *"as old as that used in the battle of Hastings"*.

It would be a logical assumption that these Indians learned to construct and use the cross-bow from the English survivors of the Lost Colony who would have known how to construct and use that weapon. The construction of the bow is not complicated and even non-military men would be able to duplicate the cross-bow.

McMillan found that from the earliest settlement by white men, the Robeson County Indians have been an English-speaking race. He describes their language as having peculiarities that are reminiscent of the English vernacular, or language of common use, popularized in the time of Geoffrey Chaucer (c. 1343-1400), with *"a number of old English words, which have become obsolete in English-speaking countries, (but) are in common use among them."*

McMillan gives examples of this unique language: "hit is used (for) it, hwing for wing, aks for ask, hosen for hose, housen for houses, lovend for loving, mension for measurement, and mon for man". This is confirmed by Dr. Stephen Weeks as quoted in **The Only Land I Know** (Dial and Eliades) in 1975. *"They have preserved many forms in good use three hundred years ago, but which are now obsolete in the written language* *and are found only in colloquial and dialectical English."* This would mean that Old English speech was characteristic among the Lumbees when they were discovered by white men in the early eighteenth century. It could be observed among the Lumbees as late as the 1950's, but has been corrupted steadily by exposure to mass media.

Many people believe that it would have been more likely that the colonists would have adopted the language of the Indians, rather than the Indians learning to speak English. The case for the supremacy of English is easy to understand by examining the drawings of John White.

The Hatteras Indians were a small tribe, with approximately a dozen families in a village. It would be reasonable to assume that Manteo's village was typical in this regard.

Therefore, the colonists joining them would have been in the majority and their language the predominant one. Also, Manteo communicated with the colonists in English, and it is logical that the other Indians would have been influenced to do the same.

Since the English dominated in architecture, fashion, and practical skills and crafts, they would naturally dominate in language as well. The various Indian groups who may have joined them had different languages, so adopting English as their common language would have established a standard for easier communication. The Lumbees say that they have always been friendly to the white men, accepting his language, religion and laws as a means of becoming great and powerful as the white men were.

It would not have been difficult for the Croatan Indians to embrace the religion of the colonists of Roanoke. As Thomas Hariot described the religion of the Indians in his *An Account of the Inhabitants and Commodities in "Virginia"*, (**Explorations, Descriptions, and Attempted Settlements of Carolina, 1584-1590**), they believed in many lesser gods, but only one *"chief and great God, which has been from all eternity"*. They believed this great God had created everything, and they believed in the immortality of the soul which will live forever either in the eternal bliss of heaven or continually burn in a pit. Accepting Christianity, especially when led by Manteo, would have been an inevitable step.

The universal tradition among the Lumbee Indians is that they descend from the Cherokees and English, and their ancestors were from *"Roanoke in 'Virginia'"*, meaning Eastern North Carolina. They describe the English of Roanoke as uniting with their tribe and being conducted to the Indian settlement on the Neuse River, then gradually moving westward to the Lumber River. The swamps surrounding the area of Robeson County, which made it undesirable to both Indians and settlers, made it the perfect hideaway for a mixed group of people seeking to withdraw from the world into their own unique culture.

They have no written history. Their past, including their arrival on the Lumber River, is preserved only in oral tradition. Their tradition also indicates that at an early time their ancestors located for a period on the mainland southwest of Pamlico Sound. They cite as tradition that their ancestors had dwelling places on the Cape Fear River as well as on tributaries of the Black River in Sampson County.

In an isolated, inland part of North Carolina buffered from intrusion by swamps, it is not hard to imagine how the lost colonists joined with the Hatteras Indians from Croatan Island, and perhaps some refugees from the Eastern Siouan Indians, to produce the English speaking Lumbee Indians encountered in 1729-1731 by the first settlers in the area.

Lumbee tradition places them in Robeson County by 1650, giving them eighty years to develop their European culture undisturbed, farming after the English manner and building English-style houses. Their Indian background was evidenced by the fact that they held all of their lands in common, without boundaries of ownership. This method served them well until the coming of the white man. With the system of grants and deeds granted by the English Crown, much Lumbee land was lost to them. Finally, the Lumbees learned that in order to keep their land they would have to accept the English law of holding title to it. The first evidence of a land grant to a Lumbee was in 1732 to Henry Berry and James Lowery. Others later purchased land from those who had been given large land grants by the crown.

McMillan makes the point that the reports of finding crosses and letters carved into the bark of trees in the area between the Neuse and Pamlico rivers (known as Secotan) supports the statement of John White that the colonists were planning to remove *"fifty miles into the main"*, since that region fits his description if the colonists set out from Croatoan Island.

Further confirming the connection of the Lumbee Indians of Robeson County with the Roanoke colonists, McMillan mentions a 200 year old (in 1888) medical book brought to North Carolina by immigrants and full of curious remedies in common use among the English of the 17th century. He found many of these remedies still in common use among the Indians of Robeson County. As well equipped for survival as Sir Walter Raleigh expected his colonists to be, it is easy to believe that such a medical book was standard equipment on all of his voyages of exploration and colonization.

The Europeans introduced epidemic diseases in America, which devastated the Indian population with no immunity to these new illnesses. There is compelling evidence of the

English heritage of the Lumbee Indians even in these epidemics. Apparently, their English heritage passed to them some natural immunity to deadly diseases, such as smallpox, which were common in Europe. As we now know, those exposed to a disease without succumbing to it, as the Roanoke colonists would have been in England, develop natural immunities. It is most interesting that while other Indian populations were severely reduced or wiped out by the diseases of the English, the percentage of Lumbee Indians who died was not nearly as great. They inherited the immunities their ancestors brought with them from England.

Something as insignificant as a grape did not escape McMillan's notice during his investigation. The scuppernong grape is a hybrid that can be propagated only by cuttings. This grape was discovered on Roanoke Island by the English in 1585. McMillan points out that this grape may be found along the old Lowery Road from the Neuse River to the Santee River in South Carolina. Since early settlers found this grape growing in the Cape Fear Region that had been occupied by the Lumbee Indians, it indicates that they had interaction with the eastern coast of North Carolina in early times.

As described in **The Only Land I Know** (Dial and Eilades), Hamilton McMillan was so convinced that at least some of the Roanoke colonists had survived and joined with Manteo's tribe to ultimately find their way to Robeson County, that he was successful in getting the North Carolina General Assembly to designate the Robeson County Indians as the "Croatan Indians". Today we know that Croatan was an erroneous designation of the Indians who occupied Croatan Island. It was actually the Hatteras Indians who lived on Croatan Island when the Lost Colony was planted. However, the importance of the designation, recognizing the descendants of the Lost Colony, is not diluted by the error in name. In 1911, the General Assembly changed the name to "Indians of Robeson County," and in 1913, the legislature designated them as the "Cherokee Indians of Robeson County".

McMillan wrote, *"My opinion is, from a very exhaustive examination… that these Indians are not only descendants of Sir Walter Raleigh's lost colony…but that they are also mixed with the Cherokee Indians."* He went on to say that *"from time immemorial"* the Lumbees have claimed to be *"of Cherokee descent and they further have a tradition among them that their ancestors, or some of them, came from Roanoke and 'Virginia'. Roanoke and 'Virginia', of course, originally comprised all of eastern North Carolina, including Roanoke Island, the settlement of Sir Walter Raleigh's lost colony."*

The Cherokee connection is easy to understand, since they traveled along the Lowery Trail to the coast and no doubt intermingled with the Indians along that route. Perhaps the new mixed culture of the Lumbee Indians appealed to them.

Many scholars have recognized the significance of the presence of so many last names found among the Lumbee Indians which are the same or similar to the list of colonists contained in John White's log of the colonists left on Roanoke Island in 1587. Of the ninety-five different surnames found among the colonists, McMillan found forty-one present among the Lumbees. Such names as Howe, Cooper, Jones, and Stevens are admittedly common English names, but it is hard to imagine how English names would show up among an isolated people more than two hundred miles from the coast. Although some of the earlier family names have disappeared over the years, McMillan found in the late nineteenth century that in excess of forty-three percent of the names on John White's log were found among the Lumbees. The most logical explanation would be a familial connection with the people of the Lost Colony. In her book, **Sacred Grounds,** Jane Blanks Barnhill mentions that the very earliest gravestones inscribed revealed both the given names and the sir names as being English names.

Because of the high incidents of surnames of the lost colonists among the Lumbee Indians today, there are DNA projects underway to match DNA of those Lumbees to Englishmen with the same or similar names. Such names as Paine, (Payne), Gibbes, (Gibbs), Berry, (Barrye), and Brooke, are examples of names listed in the log of the Lost Colony and found today among the Lumbees.

DNA testing and comparisons will take years of work, but initial results are encouraging. In a paper entitled, "Where Have All the Indians Gone?", Roberta Estes makes the following observation: *"The highest frequencies of non-hypened Native DNA found in the Bolnick (et al, 2006), and Malni (et al, 2008), studies were 47% and 88% respectively. Similar frequency of admixture would be expected within the Lumbee descendant population, but a significantly higher admixture rate is found. Of Lumbee descendants who have tested, 96% have Y-chromosomal (paternal) non-Native DNA, which is higher than either Bolnick (et al, 2006), or Malni (et al, 2008), and is suggestive either of earlier European contact or a significant infusion of European DNA, perhaps from the Lost Colony."*

An article in the Fayetteville Observer (Fayetteville, N.C.) dated May 18, 1998, referred to pockets of Croatoan Indian artifacts unearthed on Hatteras Island by the powerful storm, Emily, as it swept across the area in 1993.

In addition, Croatoan Indian artifacts were discovered along Buxton's dune ridge. Found among these artifacts were three hundred year old coins, a smoking pipe, broken wine bottles, flints and musket balls, twin hearths, copper and brass pieces, and lead droppings.

Dr. David Phelps, a marine archaeologist from East Carolina University stated, *"These findings provide the strongest*

evidence to date that the English lived among these Indians."
This is compelling evidence that the colonists were not
slaughtered, but moved to Croatoan where they were among
friends who were members of the Chawanooks tribe, whose
king, Menatonon, was reported to be a true friend of the
English. The Chawanooks were the strongest nation in the
area, with their chief town on the Chowan River. The town was
described as, *"able to put seven hundred fighting men into the
field besides the force of the province itself"*. The Chawanooks
would have been able to shelter the colonists and assist them
with their plans to settle in a permanent location.

In an article in the "Journal of Genetic Genealogy" (2009)
entitled, "Where Have All the Indians Gone?", author Roberta
Estes quotes historian James Sprunt as saying, *"The Cape
Fear Coree Indians told the English settlers of the Yeamans
colony in 1669 that their lost kindred of the Roanoke colony,
including Virginia Dare …had been adopted by the once
powerful Hatteras tribe and had become amalgamated with
the children of the wilderness. It is believed that the Croatans
of this vicinity are descendants of that race."*

In his book, **Sir Walter Raleigh's Lost Colony,** Hamilton
McMillan references a 1608 chart of Virginia (Captain Francis
Nelson) and makes the following comments: *"The legends on
this chart of the year 1608 relate to incidents which happened
within twenty-one years after the colony was left at Roanoke*

and indicate the fact that white men from Roanoke were alive at Ohanahowan on the Neuse River and at Passarapanicik (the) same region, having stone houses, two stories high, tame turkeys and other evidences of civilization, and Machumps says expressly that the people were taught to build by those English who escaped the slaughter at Roanoke. What is meant by the slaughter at Roanoke we do not know, unless the allusion is to the men left on the island to hold possession and who were never seen again. The allusion could not be to the colonists left by White, for there was no evidence that they left the island in any distress."

The men he mentions as *"left on the island to hold possession and who were never seen again"* were those fifteen men left on Roanoke Island by Sir Richard Grenville when he returned to resupply the members of the Second Voyage, but found the island completely deserted.

Captain Francis Nelson's map of 1608 apparently mistakenly identifies Ohanahowan and Passarapanicik as being on the Neuse River when John White's map places them on the Chowan River.

However, when Hamilton McMillan interviewed the aged Lumbee Indian woman in 1888, she specifically identified the Neuse River as the site to which her ancestors were conveyed by an Indian chief. If the colonists separated into groups as seems likely, some could have settled at least for a time on the Chowan River, while other groups followed the Indian chief to the Neuse River.

POINT: There is overwhelming evidence that the Roanoke colonists did not disappear, but moved inland, using rivers and a network of Indian trails to the Lumber River area of present day Robeson County in North Carolina. Hamilton McMillan reported that along the Indian trail known as the Lowery Trail, discoveries were made of construction which required more advanced skill and knowledge than the Indians possessed. He also mentioned that Indians of the area were skilled in the use of the cross-bow.The conclusion being that they would have learned the construction and use of such a weapon from the Roanoke colonists.

When the Lumbee Indians were discovered, they spoke a type of English from the age of Chaucer. This would be the English spoken by the Roanoke colonists. It is Lumbee tradition that the Roanoke colonists united with their tribe and were conducted to an Indian settlement on the Neuse River, gradually moving westward to the Lumber River. Lumbee tradition places them in the Robeson County area by 1650, giving them eighty years to develop their unique culture before the arrival of white men in the interior of North Carolina.

The Lumbee Indians claimed to have come from Eastern North Carolina They had no remnants of their Indian language that would help connect them to other tribes, but they claim descent from the survivors of the Roanoke colony. When discovered, they dressed as the English did and practiced practical skills and arts they would have learned from the Roanoke colonists. The Indians of the Roanoke area believed in one God who had created everything, and it was inevitable that they would accept the Christian religion as Manteo had done. A church was one of the discoveries Hamilton McMillan mentioned as being along the Lowery Trail. Reports of crosses carved in the bark of trees between the Neuse and Pamlico Rivers supports John White's statement that the Roanoke colonists planned to move "fifty miles into the main". That region fits the description if the colonists set out from Croatoan Island.

A two hundred year old medical book (in 1888) which was brought to N.C. by immigrants was full of curious remedies that were still in common use among the Lumbee Indians. There are many English last names found among the Lumbees that are found on the list of colonists left on Roanoke Island in 1587.

After careful consideration of the evidence in 1911, the North Carolina General Assembly officially recognized the Lumbee Indians as coming from Croatoan Island. In 1993, a hurricane unearthed Croatoan Indian artifacts on Hatteras Island. This is compelling evidence that the Roanoke colonists were not slaughtered, but lived among the Croatoan Indians.

Review the Evidence

In 1587, 118 English colonists were left on Roanoke Island in what is now the Outer Banks of North Carolina. According to written history, they were never seen by white men again. But is that true? Their fate has been an intriguing mystery for hundreds of years, but not until the late nineteenth century was any in depth search made for these brave souls who risked all to lay the foundation of the nation now known as the United States of America. Our history is full of well-researched books detailing the lives and accomplishments of so many worthy men and women involved in the founding and growth of our nation, but the colonists left on Roanoke Island have for too long received scant attention. Perhaps at the time of their "disappearance" it was not expedient to call attention to what appeared to be a failed attempt to settle America. Too much fuss over the missing colonists might have discouraged the financial backers so essential for future colonizing efforts.

Misfortune and false starts were part of any great undertaking of colonization, and the colonists of Roanoke may have been considered part of the cost of the venture. In the Age of Exploration, there were many other enterprises to divert the attention of enthusiastic adventurers from one failure.

So little investigation was done when the clues were still fresh, and the meager efforts made were so haphazard that reaching a firm conclusion today about the colonists' fate has been made more difficult than it should have been. Most hard evidence left behind has been obliterated by time and the elements, or buried deep in the earth. Those who chronicled the first English attempt at colonization in America and those who first investigated the failure are exasperatingly parsimonious in their reports. Where details seem most appropriate, the writers are most succinct. Compared to the wealth of detail included in the reports of the new country itself, the reports on the fate of the colonists showed a surprising lack of natural curiosity. There are many tantalizing hints that were never satisfactorily explored.

With so little definitive information available even today, it is necessary to take a broader view of what can be useful in determining the fate of the colonists. The primary source, the original reports, are revealing in what was included and what was not included. Sometimes what isn't reported is just as important in reaching conclusions as what is reported. Considering the source of the information and the writer's personal point of view is critical in weighing the validity of the information and placing it in the context of known facts.

Original maps and drawings of the areas of interest give additional insight and can be useful in confirming or excluding information. An understanding of the colonists and the natives is essential. With so little written history to document the fate of the colonists, it is necessary and valid to consider oral history. In the end, logical conclusions must be made where history is silent.

It is the belief of the authors of this book that there is a strong case for the survival of the colonists of Roanoke Island and their resettlement with the Croatan Indians on the banks of the Lumber River in Robeson County, North Carolina. A review of significant points supports this belief:

Based on reports of the voyages, it is clear that the Indians' first impulse was to befriend the colonists. From their initial encounter with the English, the Indians were naturally curious and impressed by the more advanced culture of the English. They understood the value of befriending people with superior skills and weapons. Ensonore, the main leader of the Indians, was a firm friend of the English until his death and influenced his subordinates to follow his lead. When mistreatment of the Indians by the English strained relations during the Second Voyage, the Indians did not respond with all the force they could have. Explorer of the 1700's, John Lawson, said of the Indians, they *"are really better to us than we have been to them"*. He also said, *"The Indians are very revengeful, and never forget an Injury done, till they have received Satisfaction."* He would not have made such a statement if he had not witnessed the Indians being mistreated by Englishmen. A very telling statement of Lawson is recorded in Hugh Talmage Lefler's **Introduction to A New Voyage to Carolina.**

Lawson wrote that the Indians *"always give us Victuals at their Quarters, and take care we are armed against Hunger* and *Thirst: We do not do so by them, (generally speaking) but let them walk by our Doors Hungry and do not often relieve them. We look upon them with Scorn and Disdain, and think them little better than Beasts in Human shape."* He also said that *"we ... daily cheat them in everything we sell, and esteem it a Gift of Christianity not to sell them so cheap as we do to the Christians as we call ourselves."*

A land owner and associate of Lawson's, Thomas Pollock, is quoted in the same book saying, *"our own devising hath been the cause of all our troubles,"* in referring to relations with the Indians.

Lawson is further quoted describing the Indians as *"apt to learn any Handicraft, as any People that the World affords... we have no disciplin'd Men in Europe, but what have, at one time or other, been branded with Mutining, and Murmuring against their Chiefs. These Savages are never found guilty of that great Crime in a Soldier; I challenge all Mankind to tell me of one Instance of it; besides, they never prove Traitors to their Native Country, but rather chuse Death than partake and side with the Enemy...They naturally possess the Righteous Man's Gift; they are Patient under all Affliction, and have a great many other Natural Vertues, which I have slightly touch'd throughout the Account of these Savages..."*

It would appear from these statements that the colonists leaving Roanoke Island would have little to fear from the Indians.

Through all of the voyages until he disappeared with the colonists, Manteo remained a loyal friend and even took the side of the English against his own people in controversies. Manteo was in the group left on Roanoke Island in 1587.

When hostilities arose, the Chowanocks, who were affiliated with Manteo and the Croatan Indians, remained friendly to the colonists who arrived in 1587. Manteo would have been able to assess whether there was any great hostility towards the colonists, other than from the small remnant of hostile Indians who had aligned with Wanchese after Wingina's death. While Fernando kept the ships anchored off shore for over a month after arriving at Roanoke, none of the colonists felt endangered enough to return to England.

There was an agreement in place before John White's departure for England that at some point the colonists would relocate fifty miles inland. Most likely they discussed various sites with Manteo who was well acquainted with the best places to settle in safety. It appears that the colonists left Roanoke in late winter or early spring of 1588. This would have been logical if they wanted to reach their new location in time to plant crops for harvest in the summer and fall.

A Spanish ship happened upon Roanoke Island in the summer of 1588, and it was reported that there was evidence of a settlement being there, but it had been deserted. There was no mention of any sign of hostilities or distress.

The physical evidence John White found upon his return indicated an organized departure of the colonists. He found nothing to alarm him, such as burned houses, bones or graves, and was convinced the colonists were safe with Manteo's people on Croatoan Island. They had left the prearranged sign of their destination.

Twenty years later, there were reports from the Jamestown colony that the Indians knew of places where white people were living with Indians. The Jamestown colonists did not make great efforts to find these white people. In 1607, George Percy described the report of an expedition where a boy with fair skin and yellow hair was sighted. There is no conclusive evidence that any of these sightings involved people from the Lost Colony, but they do provide proof of the co-existence of Indians and white people. John Smith of the Jamestown colony received the report of an Indian chief that he knew of people living in houses built like the English houses, but no one from Jamestown ever saw such houses.

In 1612, William Strachey, Secretary of the Jamestown colony, wrote a report mentioning Indian settlements with two-story stone houses which the colonists of Roanoke who survived the supposed slaughter had taught the Indians to build. This report is questionable for two reasons. First, the slaughter mentioned supposedly occurred just prior to the arrival of the Jamestown colonists at a time when the evidence shows the Roanoke colonists had long since left Roanoke Island to move inland.

The second reason is that building two-story stone houses is not a skill quickly acquired. It would have required skill in the use of advanced tools the Indians did not possess, as well as a long apprenticeship.

There would not have been sufficient time for the supposed survivors to integrate with strange Indians ignorant of advanced construction skills and teach them to build two-story stone houses. Also, it is odd that there was never any mention of colonists in the area living in stone houses. If they had remained in the area, surely they would have constructed stone houses for themselves.

An expedition from Jamestown found crosses and letters carved into the bark of trees not far from Jamestown. Was this an indication that colonists from Roanoke were living there? Probably not. Any Indian coming in contact with the colonists could have learned the use of the cross symbol as well as a few English letters. Since only "letters" were found and not words, which the English would be more likely to leave, it isn't proof that the Roanoke colonists were in the area. It is just as likely these carvings were left as markers by members of the Second Voyage on one of their expeditions into the area.

In 1663, Englishmen from Barbados explored the Cape Fear River in North Carolina and encountered Indians who were not afraid of the firing of English guns and who spoke English words of friendship and welcome to them. The Indian chief mentioned beheading as a punishment for one who had offended the Englishmen. Beheading was not an Indian form of punishment and must have been learned from contact with Englishmen. This encounter took place approximately forty miles above Wilmington at Indian Wells. This site is described by writers McMillan and Lowery as a place where the Hatteras Indians (Croatoan) and the Roanoke colonists dwelt for a time.

As early as 1690, French emigrants settling on Pamlico Sound encountered a mixed race of people they called "Melange", later known a "Malungeon". The traditions of the Croatoan Indians of Robeson County, North Carolina indicate that they had previously moved towards the southwest and settled in various places along the great trails leading from the mountains to the coast. It is possible this mixed race were descendants of the Roanoke colonists and the Croatoan Indians as they made their way inland. Perhaps some decided to stay in the area of Pamlico Sound.

John Lawson visited Hatteras Island (Croatoan Island) in 1700, and reported that the Indians told him their ancestors were white people who could read books. He said this was confirmed by the presence of gray eyes found among these particular Indians. The Indians' oral tradition was that their ancestors were the Roanoke colonists. The Indians presented him with chickens. Domestic fowl were introduced to the North American Continent by the colonists.

Lawson also reported the discovery in the town of Bath, North Carolina's oldest town, of artifacts indicating that the Roanoke colonists lived there for some period of time.

A letter dated 1703, and written by Rev. Mr. Blair, a missionary to settlements on Pamlico Sound, reports a *"great nation of Indians"* living among the English and very civilized. Rev. Blair's estimate of the size of the "nation" at 100,000 is considered an exaggeration, and his location as indefinite. But historian, Hamilton McMillan, believes this report is evidence that members of the Lost Colony were living in an area southwest of Pamlico at that time.

Mr. McMillan believed the reference was to the tribe known as Croatoans, because there was no other tribe to which it could apply. In 1703, there were no known settlements of white men beyond Pamlico Sound.

In 1729, when the first English penetrated what is now Robeson County, N.C., they found living along the Lumber River a mixed race of people dwelling in English style houses, cultivating crops, showing skill in the English arts, and speaking English in the style of the sixteenth century. Many of their surnames were found among the Roanoke colonists. This mixed-race people had no written language or history. Their oral tradition was that their forefathers were from the Lost Colony of Roanoke.

Hamilton McMillan interviewed an elderly woman, perhaps ninety-years old, of the Croatoan tribe who told him her ancestors came from *"Roanoke in 'Virginia'"*. In Croatoan tradition, Virginia refers to the area adjacent to Pamlico Sound. She further stated that the colonists were taken overland to a settlement on the Neuse River by Chief Wyonoke.

McMillan reports an incident which occurred in 1864, which affirms their tradition of friendship with the white man: *"Three young men of a Lowerie family were conscripted by the Confederate authorities to work on the batteries at Fort Fisher, and while on the road to the nearest railway station were killed, it is supposed, by the officer who had them in charge. The funeral of these young men was numerously attended by whites and Indians, and an old Indian named George Lowery, made a short address, the substance of which is as follows: 'We have always been the friends of white men. We were a free people long before the white man came to our land. Our tribe lived in Roanoke, in Virginia. When the English came to this land we treated them kindly. One of our men went to England in an English ship and saw that great country. We took the English to live with us. There is the white man's blood in these veins as well as that of the Indian. In order to be great like the English we took the white man's religion and laws, for we were told that if we did that, we would prosper. In the fights between the Indians and the white men we always fought on the side of the white men. We moved to this land and fought for liberty for white men, yet white men treated us as Negroes. Here are our young men killed by a white man and we get no justice, and that in a land where we were always free.'"* (**Sir Walter Raleigh's Lost Colony** by Hamilton McMillan, 1888).

Conclusion

Stephen B Weeks, a professional historian, examined all of the evidence, both written and oral, on the Croatan (Lumbee) Indians and summed it up in his 1891 article entitled, *The Lost Colony of Roanoke: Its Fate and Survival*, which appeared in the Papers of the American Historical Association:

"The Croatans (Lumbees) of to-day claim descent from the lost colony. Their habits, disposition, and mental characteristics show traces of Indian and European ancestry. Their language is the English of three hundred years ago, and their names are in many cases the same as those borne by the original colonists. No other theory of their origin has been advanced, and it is confidently believed that the one here proposed is logically and historically the best, supported as it is both by external and internal evidence. If this theory is rejected, then the critic must explain in some other way the origin of a people which, after the lapse of three hundred years, show the characteristics, speak the language, and possess the family names of the second English colony planted in the western world....in conclusion, it seems incontestable that the Lumbee Indians are the product of an environment that produced a swamp-surrounded island of land, which in turn afforded isolation and protection and brought together in the community remnants both of the Lost Colony and several Indian tribes, of which the Hatteras and various Eastern

Sioan were the most prominent. While there are some who will find the conclusion of amalgamation unsatisfactory, it is the only conclusion possible in light of the facts, traditions of the people and logic of the situation. The origin of the Lumbee Indains should no longer be viewed as lost."(Quoted from **The Only Land I Know, A History of the Lumbee Indians** by Adolph L. Dial and David K. Eliades).

Franklin Delano Roosevelt, visit to Fort Raleigh August 18, 1937:

"Perhaps even it is not too much to hope that documents in the old country and excavations in the new may throw some further light, however dim, on the fate of the 'lost colony', Roanoke, and Virginia Dare."

Chapter 16

The Significance of the Lost Colony
to the United States and England

In 1890, North Carolina historian, Stephen B. Weeks, presented a paper at the annual meeting of the American Historical Association. The paper was entitled "Raleigh's Settlements on Roanoke Island" and contained the following quote: *"No spot in Britain... can be so sacred to Englishmen as that which first felt the tread of English feet; and to Americans no spot should be so sacred as Roanoke Island in Dare county, North Carolina, within sight and sound of the stormy Atlantic, where the first English settlement in the new world was made... here was turned the first spade of earth to receive English seed; here the first English house was built; and here...Virginia Dare, the first of Anglo-Americans, was born."*

The 1893, May-June issue of the "Magazine of American History", contained a piece by Edward Graham Daves entitled, "Raleigh's 'New Fort in Virginia – 1585". In the article, Mr. Daves wrote that Roanoke Island *"is the starting point of events as pregnant with great results in the wonderful history of our race, as was the landing of our forefathers on the shores of Kent, when they migrated from their Holstein homes more than a thousand years before... no spot in the country should be dearer or more sacred to us than that which was marked by the first footprints of the English race in America...in these days of enthusiasm about Columbus and his explorations it is especially important not to lose sight of the fact that he did not discover the continent of North America, and that the United States owe nothing to Spanish civilization. That influence was to mould the destiny of the peoples who gathered in the new world south of the Gulf of Mexico: but Cabot with his English explorers was the first to set foot on our Atlantic coast, and it is to English enterprise, English moral standards, English political ideas, and English civil and religious liberty, that we owe the manifold blessings we now enjoy, and to which we must gratefully ascribe the marvelous progress and prosperity of our beloved country."*

Mr. Daves, like the authors, could not understand why so little was known of the historical importance to our country of Roanoke Island, while St. Augustine, Jamestown, and Plymouth were so well known.

When Senator Zebulon B. Vance made an unsuccessful attempt in 1884, to establish congressional recognition of Roanoke Island as the birth place of American civilization, he stated, *"This was the beginning of our national history."* Unfortunately, this attempt was opposed by Senator John J.

Ingalls of Kansas, who was born and reared in Massachusetts and likely did not want his home state deprived of its historical fame. The textbook historical narrative of our beginnings was by then so ingrained that no one wanted to consider a date of our origins prior to Jamestown and later the Pilgrims of Plymouth.

So it is that our history books continue to ignore the importance of the **Lost Colony of Roanoke Island** to the founding of the United States of America. While students all over the country may be able to recite the dates and facts about the settlements at Jamestown and Plymouth, few outside of North Carolina are aware of the first permanent English settlement in North America which began on Roanoke Island between 1584 and 1587, and eventually flourished in the swamps along the Lumber River in present day Robeson County, North Carolina.

Postface

The Honorable Hamilton Mcmillan
(1837 - 1916)

The Lost Colony of Roanoke disappeared from view not long after it was established in 1587, and historians paid little attention for hundreds of years until the late nineteenth century when lawyer and teacher, Hamilton McMillan took an interest. Mr. McMillan was an educated man, graduating from the University of North Carolina in 1857. Working as a teacher and a lawyer, he became increasingly fascinated with the people around Red Springs known as "Croatan Indians". His interest in history and land titles inspired his investigation into their origins.

McMillan moved with his family to Red Springs in 1883. He had a kindly disposition and preferred the quiet country life. He gained the trust of the Indians and spent much time talking to them about their oral history, as well as studying what he could find of their history. He was disturbed by their condition in society and determined to do whatever he could to lift them up. In 1885, he was elected to the North Carolina House of Representatives. During the two years he was a representative, he introduced legislation to give the Indians of Robeson County a name of their own and separate schools. During his second term as a representative, The Croatan

Normal School was established to train Indians as teachers. Later, the school would become The University of North Carolina at Pembroke.

From McMillan's extensive research and the oral history the Indians shared with him, he came to the conclusion that the Lumbee Indians were the descendants of Sir Walter Raleigh's Lost Colony of Roanoke Island.

McMillan was the first to investigate the origin of the Lumbee Indians found mainly in Robeson County, and he presented his research in a pamphlet entitled "Sir Walter Raleigh's Lost Colony". Scholars consider his pamphlet a true history of the Lumbee Indians.

McMillan is recognized as the founder of the University of North Carolina at Pembroke as a result of his efforts in establishing its foundation, the Croatan Normal School. A statue of Hamilton McMillan was unveiled on the university campus on March 5, 1987, as the school celebrated its first one hundred years.

Hamilton McMillan was many things: lawyer, scholar, educator, historian, humanitarian, legislator and Civil War veteran, but above all, he will be remembered as a true friend of the Lumbee Indians.

Addendum:
Virginia Dare's Gravesite

In a Red Springs, N.C., cotton field one mile west of historic Philadelphus Presbyterian Church stands an ancient tree encircled by undisturbed earth. Its gnarled branches perhaps shelter one of our country's great historical sites. Yet the area is unremarkable to passersby and is in no way protected or marked. According to the oral tradition of the local Lumbee Indians, this is the burial site of Virginia Dare, the first English child born in "America" in 1587. The large tree has been professionally estimated to be between 400-500 years old, which would mean it was already a mature tree when Virginia Dare would have been buried.

Two questions come to mind: First, how is it possible that this particular site has remained preserved and unmolested for hundreds of years, while all around it the fields are plowed? Second, why has nothing been done to validate the oral tradition of the Lumbee Indians regarding such a significant part of history and to ensure the continued protection of the site?

The first question is the easiest to answer. Obviously, the local people know of the oral tradition and believe or at least respect it. For hundreds of years, no one has disturbed the site. In 1938, Lamont Smith, Editor of the Wilmington

Star, wrote an article entitled *Old Indian Legend, Grave Site of Virginia Dare*, in which he reported that for generations it had been repeated that the "Great White Spirit" would frown upon those who dared molest this sacred soil.

Many of the local residents recalled parents warning them that this was a sacred Indian graveyard where they should not play. Jordan Revels, an Indian patriarch, would not state that this was definitely the grave of Virginia Dare, but he said it had long been tradition that this spot should not be despoiled. He also pointed out that the name "Dial", commonly found among Indians in Robeson County, was a corruption of the English name "Dare", and he remembered a story that the Dares came from somewhere in the distant past and settled near Philadelphus. He was also aware of the tradition of a connection between this grave and the Lost Colonists of Roanoke Island. Jordan Maynor, another aged Indian, confirmed that the story of the sacred burial spot had been a part of Lumbee tradition for generations. The patriarchs also told a story of a pale faced maiden buried there. Miss Anna Liza Buie, on whose ancestral land the site is situated, recounted how her father told his children the grave was not to be disturbed, though no one would say who lay beneath the soil. She remembered feeling that there was something special about the grave.

The second question cannot be answered satisfactorily. Although this site is the only one in the oral tradition of the

Lumbee Indians to be designated as holding the remains of a person from the Lost Colony, it has not received the attention it deserves from professional historians and archaeologists. In researching the Lost Colony, author William V. Pate, Sr., met a gentleman known to be able to locate grave sites by the use of divining rods. Although some consider this method unscientific, a similar method has been used for hundreds of years to locate underground water.

This gentleman joined Mr. Pate and several other interested citizens, walking over the site using this method for locating graves. In the process, they discovered fifteen graves aligned in the old Protestant custom of burial in the east-west position. There were no stones or markers on the graves. The Indians customarily buried their dead in earthen mounds above the ground.

Other ancient burial sites in the area have been excavated, such as Davis's Bridge, Raft Swamp and Red Springs, but for some reason it has proven impossible to pique the interest of professional archaeologists and researchers in this most interesting site. The authors have contacted various branches of the University of North Carolina and the North Carolina Department of Archives and History in an attempt to get professionals to determine the site's significance. If it is found to be an ancient burial ground, measures must be taken to ensure the site is treated with all due respect and that it is preserved and protected as part of our nation's history.

If anyone is buried there, this site deserves respect and protection. Response to our contacts have been negative. By law, the request for research and documentation necessary to confirm an historical burial site must come from the county.

It is possible that valuable artifacts and information may be lost if this area is destroyed before it attracts attention from the right sources. The Buie Lakes Plantation LLC, having received the necessary permit for sand mining on this property, promised the Robeson County Commissioners that if it were discovered during the mining operation that a graveyard existed, the operation would cease near the site. Since there are no above ground markers, the question arises as to how the mining company is to know they are destroying a grave.

Recently, important discoveries have been publicized which promise to shed light on the inland movements of the Roanoke Colony. No doubt there are more discoveries to be made. The Indian trail known today as the Lowery Road passes through Robeson County and the evidence is strong that the colonists used it to make their way to settle in the safe, secluded swamps of the Lumber River where they no doubt left behind evidence of their lives. With the strong tradition connected to this particular site in Robeson County, it warrants investigation.

Hopefully, enough interested citizens will prevail upon local and state authorities to move quickly to protect this site until professional inspection and documentation is made.

Resources

"Explorations, Descriptions and Attempted Settlements of Carolina, 1584-1590"; State Dept of Archives and History, Raleigh, NC, 1953.

"Roanoke Island-the Beginnings of English America", by David Stick, published by Univ of NC Press, Chapel Hill, NC 1983.

"Paradise Preserved-A History of the Roanoke Island Historical Assoc"; The Univ of NC Press, Chapel Hill, 1965.

"Lumbee Indians of North Carolina", by Clarence E. Lowrey, 1960.

"The Survival of the Lost Colony-the Untold Story", by William V. Pate, Sr., 2008.

"Lost Colonists-Their Fortune and Probable Fate", by David Beers Quinn, NC Dept of Cultural Resources, 1984.

"Sir Walter Raleigh's Lost Colony", by Hamilton McMillan, Edwards & Broughton Printing Co, Raleigh NC, 1888 and 1907.

"Searching for Virginia Dare", by Marjorie Hudson, Press 53, Lewisville, NC, 2007.

"The Lost Colony in Fact and Legend", by F. Roy Johnson, Johnson Publishing Co, Murfreesboro, NC, 27855, 1983.

"A New Voyage to Carolina", by John Lawson, Univ of NC Press, Chapel Hill, 1967.

"America's 400th Anniversary – Roanoke Voyages 1584-1587", by Phil Evans, Nick Hodsdon and Doug Barger, 1984.

http://.royal.gov.uk/historyofthemonarchy.com/
kingsandQueensofengland/thetudors/elizabeth.

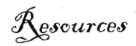

Resources

www.luminarium.org/renlit/elizabio/htm;Luminarium: Anthology of English Literature

"The Head in Edward Nugent's Hand-Roanoke's Forgotten Indians", by Michael Leroy Oberg, copyright 2008, Univ of Penn Press.

"Post Nuke" posted by James on Dec 10, 2004, Raleigh's First, "The Lost" Colony, 1585-1586.

http://tudormagic.com/thehonorable-hamilton-macmillan/hamiltonmacmillanfriendofthenativeamericans.html

"Set Fair for Roanoke-Voyages and Colonies 1584-1606", UNC Press, 1985.

"Principal Navigations-The Fourth Voyage Made to Virginia with Three Ships", by Richard Hakluyt.

"Indian Paths and Old Maps of Virginia", http://www.tradingpath.org.

"The American Indian in North Carolina", by Douglas L. Rights, John f. Blair Publisher, 1957.

"The Trading Path to the Indians", NC Historical Review Vol VIII, Pg 403, 1931.

"Time Before History: The Archaeology of NC", Stephen Davis Jr and H Trawick Ward, UNC Press, 1999.

"Where Have All the Indians Gone?", Journal of Genetic Geneology, 2009.

"Native American Eastern Seaboard Dispersal, Genealogy and DNA in Relation to Sir Walter Raleigh's Colony of Roanoke", by Roberta Estes

Resources

"The Lost City", by Shawn Miles,
www.ohio.edu/glass/vol/1/1.5.html

"Looking Back", by Julia White; (The Lumbees and the Lost Colony), www.meyra.com/lumbee.html

"Marks on the Land We Can See; Routes of Carolina's Earliest Explorers" by Tom Magnuson, NC Museum of History.

National Park Service, US Dept of the Interior, Raleigh National Historic Site, Teacher's Handbook to Roanoke Revisited

"American Colonies", www.Wikipedia.com

John Lawson, www.ucsouth.unc.edu/nc/Lawson/bio.html

"A History of the American People", by Paul Johnson "Raleigh, the Proto-American and the Roanoke Disaster", "A City on a Hill - Colonial America, 1580-1750".

Ask Jeeves Encyclopedia, www.k.ask.com/wiki

www.chroniclesofamerica.com, Sir Richard Grenville

www.nndb.com/people/963/000103654/richardgrenville

http://www.encyclopedia"Virginia".org/roanoke_colonies_ theroanokecolonies.html

"Finding the Lost Colony of Roanoke", http://skeptoid.com/episodes/4245.html

"Implosion-the Secret History of the Origins of the Lumbee Indians of Robeson County, NC", by Morris Britt, 2007.

Resources

"Captain John Smith: The Colonial Williamsburg",
www.history.org/foundation/journalsmith.cfm

"The Only Land I Know-A History of the Lumbee Indians", by Adolph L. Dial and David K. Eliades

"Algonquian Ethno-History of the Carolina Sound", by Maurice Mook; www.ncgenweb.us/hyde/ethnic/algonquin/mook3.html

"Cultural Anthropology of Indian Villages", by Fred Willard; www.lost-colony.com/cultural.html

"Poors in Tudor England",
www.tudorplace.com/ar/documents/poors.html

"Poverty in Elizabethan England", by Alexandra Briscoe, 2011; www.bbc.co.uk/history/british/tudors/poverty_01.html

"Crimes and Punishments of Poor Tudors",
www.the-tudors.org.uk/crimes-punishments-poor-tudors.html

"Tudor England", by Tiar Lambert,
www.localhistories.org/henryvii.html

"The Lost Colony's Education Pages","The People of Elizabethan England";
www.thelostcolony.org/education/students/history/
elizabethan-england.html

"If It's Not One Thing, It's Another" (weather, climate for Roanoke Colony)www.lost-colony.com/ifitsnot.html

"The Lost Colony, Chapter Two of American Slavery, American Freedom" (1975) by Edmund S. Morgan;
http://writewellgroup.com

Resources

"Between Savage Man and Most Faithful Englishman-Manteo and the Early Anglo-Indian Exchange, 1584-1590", by Michael Leroy Oberg; http://www.ncgeoweb.us/hyde/ethnic/algonquin/oberg2.html

Roanoke, the Accidental Colony; www.genpage.com/Roanoke-lost-colony.htm

http://epress.anu.edu.au

http://usersites.horrorfind.com; The Colony of Roanoke Island, Bedlam Library

Henry E. Chambers School History of the U.S. (New Orleans, F.F. Hansell and Brother 1887)